101 Ways to save money

Written by: Aiden Green

Number 1: Make a budget and stick to it

Making a budget is an essential financial planning tool that helps individuals and businesses to manage their finances effectively. It involves taking stock of your income and expenses and creating a plan for allocating your money to meet your financial goals. Here are some of the reasons why making and sticking to a budget is important:

1. Helps to control spending: A budget helps you to identify your spending habits and control your expenses, preventing overspending and unnecessary purchases.

2. Helps to save money: By setting financial goals and creating a budget, you can prioritize saving and invest in your future.

3. Provides financial discipline: Sticking to a budget requires discipline and helps to develop good spending habits that can improve your financial health.

4. Helps to identify financial problems: A budget helps you to identify areas where you are overspending and adjust your spending accordingly.

5. Helps to plan for emergencies: A budget helps you to plan for unexpected expenses and emergencies, preventing financial stress and hardship.

In conclusion, making a budget and sticking to it is essential for achieving financial stability and success. It provides a clear picture of your finances, helps to control spending, and enables you to plan for the future.

Number 2: Stop eating out and cook at home

Eating at home has become an underrated activity in our fast-paced world. With restaurants and fast food chains on every corner, eating out has become a convenient option for many people. However, there are several reasons why eating at home is better than going out to eat.

First, eating at home is more cost-effective. Cooking your meals at home allows you to control the ingredients you use, which can help you save money on groceries. Additionally, you don't have to pay for the markup on menu items, service charges, or tipping, which can add up quickly.

Second, eating at home is healthier. When you cook your meals at home, you can control the portion sizes and the ingredients you use. Restaurant meals are often high in calories, sugar, and sodium, which can lead to health problems like obesity, diabetes, and high blood pressure. Cooking at home allows you to make healthier choices and avoid these health hazards.

Third, eating at home offers more variety. When you cook at home, you can experiment with different recipes and ingredients. You can also customize your meals to suit your tastes and dietary needs. This can be difficult to do at a restaurant, where the menu options are often limited.

Fourth, eating at home provides an opportunity for family time. Cooking and eating together can help strengthen family bonds and create lasting memories. It also allows you to teach your children important life skills like budgeting, nutrition, and cooking.

Finally, eating at home is more convenient. Cooking at home can be more flexible than eating out, especially if you have a busy schedule. You can prepare meals in advance and store them in the fridge or freezer for later. This can save time and reduce stress.

In conclusion, eating at home is a better option than going out to eat. It's cost-effective, healthier, offers more variety, provides family time, and is more convenient. By cooking your meals at home, you can take control of your health, save money, and enjoy the benefits of spending time with your loved ones. So, next time you're deciding whether to go out to eat or stay in, consider the benefits of eating at home, and enjoy a home-cooked meal.

Number 3: Use coupons and shop for things on sale

In today's world, it's all about saving money and getting the best deals possible. One way to do this is by using coupons and shopping for things on sale. These simple strategies can help you stretch your budget and get the most bang for your buck.

Firstly, using coupons can save you a significant amount of money. You can find coupons for just about anything, from groceries to clothing to electronics. By taking advantage of these discounts, you can reduce your overall spending and keep more money in your pocket. You can even get coupons online, making it easier than ever to save.

Secondly, shopping for things on sale can also help you save money. Many stores have regular sales and promotions, allowing you to get the items you need at a discounted price. By taking advantage of these sales, you can save a lot of money in the long run. You can even plan your shopping trips around these sales to get the most out of your budget.

Thirdly, using coupons and shopping for things on sale can help you stretch your budget further. By reducing your overall spending, you can afford to buy more of the things you need or want. This can be especially helpful for those on a tight budget or those trying to save for a big purchase.

Fourthly, using coupons and shopping for things on sale can be a fun activity. It can feel like a game to see how much money you can save, and it can be satisfying to see the total amount saved at the end of your shopping trip. You can even make it a competition with friends or family members to see who can save the most.

Finally, using coupons and shopping for things on sale can help you become a more mindful and intentional shopper. It forces you to think about what you're buying and why, rather than just making impulse purchases. This can lead to more mindful spending habits and a greater appreciation for the things you have.

In conclusion, using coupons and shopping for things on sale is an excellent way to save money and get the most out of your budget. Not only can it help you reduce your overall spending, but it can also be a fun and satisfying activity. So next time you're headed to the store, take a few minutes to look for coupons or check out the sales. You might be surprised at how much you can save!

Number 4: Cancel subscriptions & memberships not in use

it's all too easy to sign up for subscriptions and memberships, only to forget about them or never use them. From streaming services to gym memberships, these recurring charges can quickly add up and drain your bank account. That's why it's important to regularly review your subscriptions and memberships and cancel those that you don't use.

Firstly, canceling subscriptions and memberships that you don't use can save you a significant amount of money. These recurring charges can add up quickly, especially if you have multiple subscriptions or memberships that you don't use regularly. By canceling these unnecessary expenses, you can free up money in your budget for things that you need or want.

Secondly, canceling subscriptions and memberships that you don't use can help you simplify your life. These recurring charges can clutter up your finances and make it difficult to keep track of your expenses. By canceling these unnecessary expenses, you can streamline your finances and make it easier to manage your money.

Thirdly, canceling subscriptions and memberships that you don't use can help you become more intentional with your spending. It forces you to think about what you're using and what's important to you. This can lead to more mindful spending habits and a greater appreciation for the things you have.

Fourthly, canceling subscriptions and memberships that you don't use can be a freeing experience. It can feel liberating to let go of things that are no longer serving you and simplify your life. It can also be a reminder to be more intentional with your future purchases and to only sign up for subscriptions or memberships that you know you will use regularly.

Finally, canceling subscriptions and memberships that you don't use can be a responsible financial decision. It's important to be mindful of your finances and to only spend money on things that are important to you. By canceling these unnecessary expenses, you can take control of your finances and make sure that you're not wasting money on things that you don't need or want.

In conclusion, canceling subscriptions and memberships that you don't use is an important step toward financial freedom and mindfulness. It can help you save money, simplify your life, become more intentional with your spending, and make responsible financial decisions. So take a few minutes to review your subscriptions and memberships today and cancel those that you don't use.

Number 5: Use cash instead of credit cards

Credit cards have become an essential tool for making purchases. They offer convenience and security, but they also come with risks such as overspending and accumulating debt. That's why it's worth considering the benefits of using cash instead of credit cards.

One of the most significant advantages of using cash is that it helps you stay within your budget. When you have a limited amount of money, you are more likely to think twice before making a purchase. You'll have a better idea of how much you can afford to spend, and you won't be tempted to overspend. With a credit card, it's easy to lose track of your spending, and before you know it, you've racked up a large debt.

Another advantage of using cash is that it helps you avoid interest charges. Credit card companies charge interest on the amount you borrow, and if you don't pay off your balance in full each month, those charges can add up quickly. With cash, you don't have to worry about paying interest or fees.

Using cash also offers more privacy than using credit cards. When you use a credit card, your transactions are recorded and tracked, which can be a concern for some people. If you prefer to keep your financial transactions private, using cash is a better option.

Using cash can also help you develop better financial habits. When you pay with cash, you are more aware of your spending, and you may be more likely to think about the long-term consequences of your purchases. You'll also be more likely to save money for big purchases, rather than relying on credit.

Of course, there are some downsides to using cash. For one, it can be inconvenient. You'll have to carry cash with you wherever you go, and you'll need to make sure you have enough on hand to make purchases. You'll also need to be careful not to lose your money or have it stolen.

Another drawback of using cash is that you won't be able to take advantage of rewards programs or cashback offers that credit cards often offer. If you're someone who likes to earn rewards for your purchases, using cash may not be the best choice for you.

In conclusion, while credit cards may seem like the more convenient choice, there are many benefits to using cash. It can help you stay within your budget, avoid interest charges, and develop better financial habits. If you're willing to put in the extra effort, using cash can be a smart choice for managing your finances.

Number 6: Buy generic instead of name brand

As consumers, we are often bombarded with advertisements for name-brand products. From clothing to food to electronics, the allure of name brands is often hard to resist. However, opting for generic brands can have numerous benefits, including cost savings, comparable quality, and sustainability.

One of the most obvious benefits of buying generic brands is cost savings. Generic brands are often much cheaper than their name-brand counterparts. This is because generic brands do not have to spend as much on advertising and marketing, which can be a significant cost for name brands. Additionally, generic brands often use less expensive packaging, which can further reduce costs.

Despite the lower price point, generic brands often offer comparable quality to name brands. Many generic brands are made by the same manufacturers as name brands but are simply packaged differently. This means that consumers can save money without sacrificing quality.

Another benefit of buying generic brands is sustainability. Many generic brands prioritize sustainable practices, such as using environmentally-friendly materials and reducing waste. Additionally, buying generic brands can reduce the demand for name-brand products, which can help to reduce the environmental impact of the manufacturing and transportation of those products.

In conclusion, there are numerous benefits to buying generic brands instead of name brands. Not only can consumers save money, but they can also enjoy comparable quality and support sustainable practices. Next time you are shopping, consider opting for a generic brand and see the benefits for yourself.

Number 7: Quit smoking and drinking

Many people are aware that drinking alcohol and smoking cigarettes can be harmful to their health, but what they may not realize is that these habits can also be detrimental to their finances. Quitting drinking and smoking can save a significant amount of money in the long run.

Let's start with drinking. The cost of alcohol varies depending on where you live and what you drink, but it's safe to say that it can add up quickly. A night out with friends can easily cost $50 or more, and if you do that once a week, you're looking at $200 a month. If you're a daily drinker, the costs are even higher. A bottle of wine or a six-pack of beer every day can cost you over $200 a month.

In addition to the direct costs of alcohol, there are also indirect costs. Drinking can lead to poor decisions, such as drunk driving or buying things you don't need while under the influence. These mistakes can cost you even more money.

Now let's talk about smoking. Cigarettes are expensive, and the cost is only going up. A pack of cigarettes can cost anywhere from $5 to $15, depending on where you live. If you smoke a pack a day, you're spending at least $150 a month. And that's just the direct cost.

Smoking also has indirect costs. It can lead to health problems that require medical attention, which can be expensive. It can also lead to missing work, which can result in lost wages.

If you quit drinking and smoking, you can save a significant amount of money each month. Depending on how much you're spending on these habits, you could save hundreds of dollars a month. Over a year, that adds up to thousands of dollars.

Not only will quitting drinking and smoking save you money, but it will also improve your health. Drinking and smoking are both linked to a variety of health problems, including cancer, heart disease, and liver damage. By quitting, you'll reduce your risk of these diseases and improve your overall health.

Quitting drinking and smoking isn't easy, but the benefits are well worth it. Not only will you save money, but you'll also improve your health and quality of life. There are many resources available to help you quit, such as support groups, counseling, and medication. Talk to your healthcare provider for more information on how to quit.

Number 8: Turn off lights & unplug electronic devices

Are you tired of paying high electricity bills every month? One simple solution is to turn off the lights and unplug unused electronics in your house. It may seem like a small change, but it can make a big difference in your wallet. Let's take a look at how much you can save by making these simple adjustments.

Turning off the Lights

According to the U.S. Department of Energy, lighting accounts for about 10% of your home's energy use. By turning off the lights when you leave a room, you can save up to $75 per year on your electricity bill. If you have a large house with many rooms, the savings can be even greater.

Another way to save money on lighting is to switch to energy-efficient light bulbs, such as LED bulbs. They use up to 75% less energy than traditional incandescent bulbs and can last up to 25 times longer. While they may cost more upfront, they can save you money in the long run.

Unplugging Unused Electronics

Many of us have a habit of leaving our electronics plugged in even when we're not using them. This includes devices like TVs, computers, and chargers. However, these devices still draw power even when they're not in use, which can add up over time.

According to the Lawrence Berkeley National Laboratory, standby power can account for up to 10% of your home's electricity use. By unplugging unused electronics, you can save up to $100 per year on your electricity bill. This is especially true for devices with large power adapters, such as gaming consoles and home theater systems.

Another option is to use smart power strips, which automatically turn off power to devices when they're not in use. These can be a convenient and effective way to save money on your electricity bill.

In conclusion, turning off the lights and unplugging unused electronics may seem like small changes, but they can add up to significant savings over time. By making these adjustments, you can reduce your energy use and lower your electricity bill. So, next time you leave a room or finish using a device, remember to turn off the lights and unplug them.

Number 9: Carpool or use public transportation

Both carpooling and public transportation have numerous benefits, including:

1. Cost savings

One of the biggest benefits of carpooling and taking public transportation is cost savings. When you share a ride with others, you split the cost of gas, tolls, and parking fees. Public transportation is also a lot cheaper than driving your vehicle, especially if you don't have to pay for parking. This can lead to significant savings over time.

2. Reduced pollution

Cars are one of the biggest contributors to air pollution. Carpooling and public transportation help reduce the number of cars on the road, which in turn reduces the amount of pollution being released into the air. This is a great way to reduce your carbon footprint and contribute towards a cleaner environment.

3. Less traffic congestion

The more cars there are on the road, the more traffic congestion there is. Carpooling and public transportation help reduce traffic congestion by taking cars off the road. This means less time stuck in traffic and more time to do the things you enjoy.

4. Increased social interaction

Carpooling and public transportation provide opportunities for increased social interaction. When you carpool, you get to know your fellow passengers and may even make new friends. Public transportation also provides opportunities to meet new people and engage in conversations.

In conclusion, carpooling and taking public transportation are great options for those looking to save money, reduce their carbon footprint, and enjoy a more social commute. While they may require some adjustments to your daily routine, the benefits are well worth it. So why not give it a try and see how it improves your daily commute?

Number 10: Sell items that you no longer need or use

Here are the Benefits of selling items you no longer need or use:

1. Declutter your home: One of the main benefits of selling items you no longer need or use is that it helps you declutter your home. By getting rid of items that are taking up space, you can create a more organized and comfortable living space.

2. Earn some extra cash: Selling items you no longer need or use is also a great way to earn some extra cash. You can use the money you earn to pay off debt, save for a vacation, or invest in something you've been wanting to buy.

3. Reduce waste: By selling your unwanted items, you are also helping to reduce waste. Instead of throwing things away, you are giving them a second life and keeping them out of landfills.

Tips for selling items you no longer need or use

1. Determine the value of your items: Before you start selling your items, it's important to determine their value. You can do this by researching similar items on online marketplaces or by getting an appraisal from a professional. This will help you set a fair price for your items.

2. Choose the right platform: There are many different platforms you can use to sell your items, including online marketplaces like eBay and Craigslist, social media platforms like Facebook Marketplace, and specialty websites like Etsy. Choose the platform that best fits your needs and the type of item you are selling.

3. Take good photos: When selling items online, it's important to take good photos that show the item in the best possible light. Use natural lighting and take photos from multiple angles to give potential buyers a clear idea of what they are buying.

4. Write a detailed description: Along with good photos, it's important to write a detailed description of the item you are selling. Include information like the brand, size, condition, and any other relevant details that will help potential buyers make an informed decision.

In conclusion, selling items you no longer need or use is a great way to declutter your home and earn some extra cash. By following these tips, you can successfully sell your unwanted items and enjoy the benefits of a more organized and clutter-free home.

Number 11: Shop at thrift stores and garage sales

Thrift stores and garage sales are excellent places to find amazing deals on items you need or want. Not only are they affordable, but they also offer a unique shopping experience. Here are some tips on how to make the most out of your thrift store and garage sale shopping:

1. Know what you're looking for

Before you head out to the thrift store or garage sale, have an idea of what you're looking for. It's easy to get sidetracked and buy things you don't need, so having a list of items you want to find will help you stay on track.

2. Check for quality

When shopping at a thrift store or garage sale, it's essential to check for the quality of the items you're interested in. Inspect the clothes for any stains or rips, and ensure that the electronics are in working condition.

3. Haggle for a better price

Thrift stores and garage sales are places where you can haggle for better prices. Don't be afraid to ask for a lower price, especially if you're buying multiple items. If the seller isn't willing to negotiate, you can still decide whether the item is worth the asking price.

4. Go early

If you're looking for the best deals, it's best to go early. Thrift stores and garage sales tend to have the best items available in the morning, so make sure you arrive early to get first dibs.

5. Be patient

Thrift store and garage sale shopping require patience. You may have to sift through a lot of items before you find what you're looking for, but it's worth it in the end. Take your time and enjoy the experience.

In conclusion, thrift stores and garage sales are excellent places to find amazing deals on items you need or want. By following these tips, you can make the most out of your shopping experience and score some great finds. Happy shopping!

Number 12: Repair or reuse items instead of buying new

it's easy to fall into the trap of constantly buying new items. We are bombarded with advertisements and encouraged to upgrade to the latest and greatest products. However, this mindset not only harms our wallets but also the environment. Repairing and reusing items is a sustainable and cost-effective way to reduce waste and save money.

One of the first steps to repairing and reusing items is to assess what you already have. Take inventory of the items in your home and determine what can be repaired or repurposed. For example, if a piece of furniture has a broken leg, consider repairing it rather than buying a new one. If an article of clothing has a small tear, learn how to patch it up instead of throwing it away.

There are many resources available to help you repair and repurpose items. YouTube is a great place to find tutorials on how to fix or update items. Local repair shops and tailors can also help with repairs. Additionally, there are many online communities focused on repairing and repurposing items, such as Freecycle and Craigslist.

Repurposing items is another way to reduce waste and save money. For example, an old shirt can be turned into a cleaning rag or a piece of fabric for a craft project. An old dresser can be repurposed into a bathroom vanity. The possibilities are endless.

By repairing and reusing items, we can reduce the amount of waste we produce and save money in the process. It's a win-win situation. So next time you are tempted to buy something new, consider repairing or repurposing something you already have.

Your wallet and the environment will thank you!

Number 13: Buy frequently used items in bulk

As a consumer, you likely have items that you constantly use on a daily or weekly basis. These could be anything from toiletries to household items to food staples. One way to save money and time is to buy these items in bulk, rather than purchasing them individually.

Buying in bulk has several advantages. Firstly, it can save you money in the long run. When you purchase items in bulk, you typically pay a lower price per unit compared to buying them individually. This is because manufacturers and retailers can offer discounts on larger quantities due to reduced packaging and shipping costs.

Additionally, buying in bulk can save you time and reduce the frequency of your shopping trips. Rather than having to run to the store every time you run out of a particular item, you'll have a stockpile on hand to last you for weeks or even months.

So, what items should you consider buying in bulk? Here are a few examples:

Toiletries: Items like toilet paper, soap, shampoo, and toothpaste are all things that you'll inevitably need to restock regularly. Buying in bulk can save you money and ensure that you never run out of these essentials.

Household items: Cleaning supplies, trash bags, and paper towels are all household items that you'll use frequently. Buying them in bulk can save you money and reduce the frequency of your trips to the store.

Food staples: Non-perishable food staples like rice, pasta, canned goods, and snacks are all great items to buy in bulk. Not only will you save money, but you'll also have a well-stocked pantry for those times when you don't feel like grocery shopping.

When buying in bulk, it's important to keep a few things in mind. First, make sure you have enough storage space for the items you're buying. You don't want to end up with a stockpile of toilet paper taking over your entire closet. Additionally, be mindful of expiration dates and only buy what you know you'll use before it goes bad.

In conclusion, buying in bulk for items you constantly use can be a great way to save money and time. Consider taking a closer look at the items you regularly purchase and see if there are any opportunities to buy in larger quantities.

Number 14: Use free entertainment options

It's refreshing to know that there are still free entertainment options available to us. Libraries and parks are two such options that are not just free but also offer numerous benefits.

Libraries are a treasure trove of knowledge and entertainment. They offer access to books, magazines, newspapers, movies, music, and more. Whether you're looking for a novel to get lost in or a documentary to educate yourself, the library has it all. And the best part is that you don't have to spend a dime to borrow any of these materials.

In addition to the traditional book and media offerings, many libraries also offer free classes and workshops. These can range from computer skills to crafting to cooking, allowing you to learn new skills and hobbies without spending a penny.

Parks, on the other hand, provide a natural escape from the hustle and bustle of everyday life. They offer a chance to relax, exercise, and connect with nature. Whether you prefer hiking, biking, or simply lounging in the sun, parks have something for everyone.

Many parks also offer free events and activities throughout the year. From concerts and festivals to movie nights and fitness classes, there's always something happening in the park. And unlike paid entertainment options, these events are usually family-friendly and accessible to everyone.

Using free entertainment options like libraries and parks not only saves money but also offers numerous benefits for your mental and physical health. Reading and learning new things can improve cognitive function and reduce stress while spending time in nature has been linked to improved mood and decreased anxiety.

So, the next time you're looking for something to do, consider heading to your local library or park. You'll be surprised at how much fun you can have without spending a dime.

Number 15: Purchase items during off-season or clearance sales

There are several advantages to purchasing items during off-season or clearance sales. Firstly, you can get items at a fraction of their original cost. Retailers usually offer steep discounts during these sales to move their inventory quickly. This means that you can get the same quality product at a much lower price.

Secondly, you can take advantage of the larger selection of products available during these sales. During the off-season, retailers stock up on products that are not in high demand. This means that you can find items that may not be available during peak season.

Thirdly, you can avoid the crowds that usually come with peak season shopping. During off-season and clearance sales, there are usually fewer people shopping, which means you can shop at your own pace without having to fight for space or deal with long lines.

However, there are a few things to keep in mind when shopping during off-season or clearance sales. Firstly, make sure to do your research beforehand to know which items you want to purchase and their original prices. This will help you determine if the discount being offered is worth it.

Secondly, check the item thoroughly before purchasing it. Items sold during clearance sales may have slight defects or imperfections. Make sure to inspect the product carefully before making the purchase.

Lastly, be prepared to be flexible with sizes or color options. During the off-season or clearance sales, popular sizes or colors may not be available. Be open to trying out different sizes or colors to get the best deal.

In conclusion, shopping during off-season or clearance sales is a great way to save money on purchases. By being prepared and flexible, you can take advantage of the discounts offered and get quality products at a fraction of their original price.

Number 16: Adjusting thermostat/ using energy-efficient appliances

As the cost of living continues to rise, households are always looking for ways to save money. One area that can have a significant impact on monthly expenses is utility bills. By making a few simple adjustments, households can lower their energy consumption and reduce their utility bills.

One of the most effective ways to cut down on utility bills is by adjusting the thermostat. Many households keep their homes at a constant temperature, regardless of the time of day or who is home. However, this can be wasteful and result in unnecessary heating and cooling costs. Instead, households can adjust the thermostat to match their daily routine. During the day when everyone is at work or school, the temperature can be set a few degrees higher or lower, depending on the season. When everyone is home, the thermostat can be set to a more comfortable temperature. Additionally, households can invest in a programmable thermostat that can automatically adjust the temperature based on the time of day and day of the week.

Another way to cut down on utility bills is by using energy-efficient appliances. Many households have appliances that are outdated and use a lot of energy. By replacing these appliances with newer, more energy-efficient models, households can reduce their energy consumption and save money in the long run. Appliances such as refrigerators, washing machines, and dishwashers all have energy-efficient options that can significantly lower utility bills.

In addition to adjusting the thermostat and using energy-efficient appliances, households can also make small changes to their daily routine to reduce energy consumption. For example, turning off lights when leaving a room, unplugging electronics when they are not in use, and using natural light instead of artificial light can all help lower energy consumption and reduce utility bills.

Overall, cutting down on utility bills is achievable with a few small adjustments. By adjusting the thermostat, using energy-efficient appliances, and making small changes to daily routines, households can significantly reduce their energy consumption and save money on their utility bills.

Number 17: Use a credit card with cash-back rewards

Credit cards with cash-back rewards have become increasingly popular among consumers in recent years. These cards offer a percentage of cash back on purchases made with the card, allowing consumers to earn money as they spend. The idea of earning money while spending money may sound too good to be true, but it is entirely possible with cash-back credit cards.

Using a credit card with cash-back rewards is relatively simple. The first step is to apply for a cash-back credit card that suits your needs. There are many different types of cashback credit cards available, each with its unique rewards structure. Some cards offer a flat cash-back rate on all purchases, while others offer higher rewards on specific categories like groceries, gas, or dining.

Once you have been approved for a cash-back credit card, the next step is to start using it to make purchases. When you use your card to buy something, the cashback reward is automatically applied to your account. The amount of cash back you earn depends on the rewards rate of your card and the amount of money you spend.

For example, if your cash-back credit card offers a 1% cash-back rate on all purchases, and you spend $1,000 on the card in a month, you would earn $10 in cash-back rewards. If your card offers a higher cashback rate on specific categories, like 5% on groceries, you could earn even more rewards by using your card to pay for your weekly grocery shopping.

To maximize your cash-back rewards, it is essential to use your credit card responsibly. This means paying your balance in full and on time each month to avoid interest charges. It also means avoiding overspending and only using your card for purchases you can afford to pay off.

Another way to earn even more cashback rewards is to take advantage of sign-up bonuses and promotional offers. Many cash-back credit cards offer bonuses when you sign up for the card or spend a certain amount within the first few months. Some cards also offer additional rewards for using your card to purchase from specific retailers or during specific times of the year, like the holiday season.

Using a credit card with cash-back rewards can be an excellent way to earn extra money while making everyday purchases. However, it is essential to remember that credit cards are not free money and must be used responsibly to avoid debt and financial trouble. If used wisely, a cash-back credit card can be a valuable tool for earning rewards and managing your finances.

Number 18: Bring your lunch to work or school

Bringing your lunch to work or school is a great way to save money, eat healthier, and have more control over what you eat. It may take a little extra effort, but the benefits are well worth it.

First and foremost, bringing your lunch saves money. Eating out every day can quickly add up, especially if you're buying expensive lunches or going to restaurants. Packing your lunch can cost as little as a few dollars a day, depending on what you bring. You can also buy food in bulk and prepare meals in advance to save even more money.

Another benefit of bringing your lunch is that you have more control over what you eat. When you eat out, you don't always know what's in your food or how it was prepared. By packing your lunch, you can choose the ingredients and ensure that they are fresh and healthy. You can also avoid unhealthy additives, excess salt and sugar, and other ingredients that may not be good for you.

In addition to being healthier, bringing your lunch can also be more convenient. You don't have to worry about finding a place to eat, waiting in line, or rushing back to work or class. You can eat at your own pace, in the comfort of your own space, and at a time that's convenient for you.

To make the most of your packed lunch, there are a few tips to keep in mind. First, invest in a good lunchbox or container that will keep your food fresh and at the right temperature. Consider getting a container with separate compartments to keep different foods from touching and mixing. You can also use reusable containers or bags to reduce waste and save money.

Next, plan your meals to ensure that you have enough food for the week. This can help you avoid last-minute trips to the store or resorting to unhealthy snacks. You can also prepare meals in advance, such as salads, sandwiches, or soups, and store them in the fridge or freezer until you're ready to eat them.

Finally, be creative with your meals and try new recipes. Packing your lunch doesn't have to be boring or repetitive. You can experiment with different ingredients, spices, and flavors to keep things interesting. You can also get inspiration from cookbooks, blogs, or social media.

In conclusion, bringing your lunch to work or school is a smart and healthy choice. It can save you money, give you more control over what you eat, and be more convenient than eating out. With a little planning and creativity, you can enjoy delicious and nutritious meals every day.

Number 19: Use a programmable thermostat to save money

Here are some tips on how to use a programmable thermostat to save on heating and cooling costs:

1. Choose the right thermostat

When choosing a programmable thermostat, consider the size of your home and the type of HVAC system you have. Make sure the thermostat is compatible with your system and has the features you need. There are many different types of programmable thermostats, including basic models that allow you to set a schedule for your heating and cooling, and more advanced models that can be controlled from a smartphone app and can learn your preferences over time.

2. Set a schedule

The key to saving money with a programmable thermostat is to set a schedule that matches your daily routine. For example, if you're at work during the day, you can set the thermostat to lower the temperature while you're away and raise it when you're home. Similarly, if you're going to be away on vacation, you can set the thermostat to a lower temperature to save energy.

3. Use the "away" setting

Most programmable thermostats have an "away" setting that allows you to set a lower temperature when you're not home. This can save you a significant amount of money on your heating and cooling bills. If you're going to be away for an extended period, you can also turn off the HVAC system completely to save even more energy.

4. Don't override the settings

One common mistake homeowners make with programmable thermostats is manually overriding the settings. For example, if you're feeling cold, you might turn up the heat even though the thermostat is set to a lower temperature. This can negate the energy savings you would have achieved with the programmed schedule. Instead, dress appropriately for the temperature and allow the thermostat to do its job.

In conclusion, a programmable thermostat is an easy and effective way to save money on your heating and cooling bills. By setting a schedule that matches your daily routine and using the "away" setting, you can significantly reduce your energy use and save money. Remember to choose the right thermostat for your needs, avoid overriding the settings, and monitor your energy use to achieve the best results.

Number 20: Use free online resources

One of the biggest advantages of using free online resources is the flexibility they offer. Unlike traditional classes or consulting sessions, online resources can be accessed from anywhere at any time. This makes it easier for people with busy schedules to fit learning into their daily routines. Whether you have a full-time job, family commitments, or other responsibilities, you can access online resources whenever you have a spare moment.

Another advantage of using free online resources is the cost savings. Traditional classes or consulting sessions can be expensive, with fees ranging from hundreds to thousands of dollars. Online resources, on the other hand, are often free or low-cost. This means that you can learn new skills without breaking the bank.

One of the biggest challenges of using free online resources is finding the right ones. With so many resources available, it can be overwhelming to decide which ones to use. However, there are several strategies you can use to find the best resources for your needs.

First, start by identifying your learning goals. What skills do you want to learn or improve? Once you have a clear idea of what you want to achieve, you can start looking for resources that align with your goals.

Second, look for resources that are reputable and reliable. Check the credentials of the author or creator of the resource and read reviews from other users. You want to make sure that the information you are learning is accurate and up-to-date.

Third, consider the format of the resource. Some people prefer video tutorials, while others prefer written guides or interactive exercises. Choose a format that works best for you and your learning style.

Finally, don't be afraid to try different resources and approaches. Learning is a process, and you may need to try several resources before you find the one that works best for you.

In conclusion, using free online resources is a great way to learn new skills or improve existing ones. The flexibility, cost savings, and variety of topics and expertise make online resources a valuable alternative to traditional classes or consulting sessions. By identifying your learning goals, finding reputable resources, and trying different approaches, you can take advantage of the many benefits of free online resources.

Number 21: Use a water filter instead of buying bottled water

Why Choose a Water Filter?

There are many reasons why you should consider using a water filter instead of buying bottled water. One of the most significant benefits is that it can save you money. Bottled water can be expensive, especially if you drink a lot of it. In contrast, a water filter can be purchased for a one-time cost and can last for many years with proper care and maintenance.

Another benefit of using a water filter is that it is more environmentally friendly. Plastic water bottles are a significant source of waste, and they can take hundreds of years to break down in a landfill. By using a water filter, you can reduce the amount of plastic waste that you generate and help protect the environment.

In addition to being cost-effective and environmentally friendly, using a water filter can also provide health benefits. Municipal water supplies are treated with chemicals to kill bacteria and other contaminants, but these chemicals can leave behind a residue that can be harmful to your health. A water filter can remove these chemicals, as well as other impurities such as lead, chlorine, and sediment, making your drinking water safer and healthier.

Types of Water Filters

There are many types of water filters available on the market, each with its strengths and weaknesses. Some of the most common types of water filters include:

1. Pitcher Filters: These filters are the most basic and affordable type of water filter. They fit into a pitcher and use activated carbon to remove impurities from the water. While they are effective at removing some contaminants, they may not be as effective as other types of filters.

2. Faucet-Mounted Filters: These filters attach directly to your faucet and use activated carbon to remove impurities from the water. They are more effective than pitcher filters, but they may not fit all types of faucets.

3. Counter-Top Filters: These filters sit on your counter and connect to your faucet with a hose. They are more effective than pitcher filters and faucet-mounted filters, but they take up more space on your counter.

4. Under-Sink Filters: These filters are installed under your sink and connect to your faucet with a separate tap. They are the most effective type of water filter and can remove a wide range of contaminants, but they are also the most expensive.

Number 22: Cut down on meat and eat plant-based food

The world is changing, and so are our dietary habits. People are becoming more aware of the impact their food choices have on the environment, and as a result, many are cutting down on meat consumption and eating more plant-based meals.

There are many reasons why people are making this shift. One of the main reasons is the impact that livestock farming has on the environment. Livestock farming accounts for a significant amount of greenhouse gas emissions, which contribute to climate change. By reducing our meat consumption, we can help to reduce these emissions and slow down the effects of climate change.

Another reason why people are turning to plant-based diets is for health reasons. Plant-based diets have been shown to lower the risk of chronic diseases such as heart disease, diabetes, and cancer. This is because plant-based foods are typically lower in saturated fat and higher in nutrients such as fiber, vitamins, and minerals.

Cutting down on meat and eating more plant-based meals doesn't mean you have to give up meat altogether. It's about finding a balance that works for you and your lifestyle. You could try swapping out meat for plant-based alternatives such as tofu, tempeh, or seitan. You could also try reducing your portion sizes of meat and increasing your portion sizes of vegetables and grains.

There are many delicious plant-based meals that you can try. Some of the most popular plant-based meals include salads, stir-fries, soups, and curries. There are also many plant-based snacks and desserts that you can enjoy, such as hummus, fruit smoothies, and vegan chocolate cake.

If you're not sure where to start with plant-based eating, there are many resources available to help you. There are plenty of cookbooks, blogs, and websites dedicated to plant-based eating, and many restaurants now offer plant-based options on their menus.

In conclusion, cutting down on meat and eating more plant-based meals is a positive step for both our health and the environment. It doesn't mean you have to give up meat altogether, but rather find a balance that works for you. By making small changes to our diets, we can all make a big difference in the world we live in.

Number 23: Dry clothes on a clothesline instead of the dryer

Drying clothes on a clothesline instead of a dryer is an age-old practice that has been used by people for centuries. With the advancements in technology, people have started relying more on dryers to dry their clothes. However, drying clothes on a clothesline has its own set of benefits that cannot be ignored.

One of the biggest advantages of drying clothes on a clothesline is the cost-effectiveness. Using a dryer can be expensive in the long run as it consumes a lot of electricity. On the other hand, drying clothes on a clothesline does not require any electricity, making it a cost-effective option. Moreover, by using a clothesline, you are also contributing to the environment by reducing your carbon footprint.

Another benefit of using a clothesline is that it is gentler on your clothes. Dryers use heat, which can be harsh on clothes and can cause shrinkage and fading. Hanging clothes on a clothesline allows them to dry naturally, which is much gentler on the fabric. This can help prolong the life of your clothes and prevent them from getting damaged.

Drying clothes on a clothesline can also be beneficial for your health. Dryers can accumulate lint and other particles, which can irritate allergies and cause respiratory problems. By using a clothesline, you avoid these issues and have fresh, clean air drying your clothes.

Using a clothesline can also be a fun activity for the whole family. It can be a great way to get some fresh air and spend time outdoors while doing a chore. It can also be a great opportunity for children to learn about the importance of taking care of their clothes and the environment.

In conclusion, drying clothes on a clothesline instead of a dryer has many benefits that cannot be ignored. It is a cost-effective, gentle, and environmentally friendly option that can also be a fun activity for the whole family. So the next time you have some laundry to do, try using a clothesline instead of a dryer and see the difference for yourself.

Number 24: DIY home repairs instead of hiring professionals

Home repairs are an inevitable part of homeownership. From leaky faucets to creaky floorboards, there's always something that needs fixing. While hiring a professional may seem like the easiest solution, it can also be costly. However, with the right tools and a little bit of know-how, you can save money and learn new skills by doing DIY home repairs.

Here are some common home repairs that you can do yourself:

Fixing a Leaky Faucet

A leaky faucet can be annoying and wasteful. Fortunately, fixing it is relatively simple. Start by turning off the water supply to the faucet. Next, remove the handle and the cartridge or ball valve. Clean any debris or mineral buildup from the valve and replace any worn or damaged parts. Finally, reassemble the faucet and turn the water supply back on.

Replacing a Light Fixture

Replacing a light fixture can be an easy way to update the look of a room. Turn off the power to the fixture at the circuit breaker and remove the old fixture. Follow the manufacturer's instructions to install the new fixture, making sure to connect the wires correctly. Turn the power back on and test the fixture to ensure it's working properly.

Unclogging a Drain

A clogged drain can be a frustrating issue. However, you can often clear it yourself using a plunger or a drain snake. Start by removing any debris from the drain. If using a plunger, place it over the drain and push down and up several times to create suction. If using a drain snake, insert it into the drain and turn it clockwise while pushing it through the clog. Once the clog is cleared, run hot water down the drain to ensure it's fully cleared.

Repairing a Creaky Floorboard

Creaky floorboards can be a nuisance, but they're also relatively easy to fix. First, locate the squeaky area by walking on the floor and listening for the sound. Once you've located the area, secure the floorboard to the joist below using screws.

In conclusion, DIY home repairs can be a great way to save money and learn new skills. With the right tools and a little bit of know-how, you can tackle many common home repairs yourself. However, it's important to know your limits and when to call in a professional.

Number 25: Use reusable bags instead of plastic bags

Plastic bags are a significant source of pollution and environmental damage. They take hundreds of years to decompose, and during that time, they can harm wildlife, clog waterways, and contribute to climate change. In addition, producing plastic bags requires a significant amount of energy and resources, further contributing to environmental degradation.

Reusable bags, on the other hand, are an eco-friendly alternative to plastic bags. They are made from durable materials like cotton, canvas, or recycled plastics and can be used over and over again. They come in a variety of sizes and styles, so you can choose the one that best suits your needs.

Using reusable bags is easy. Simply bring them with you whenever you go shopping, and use them instead of plastic bags. Many stores now offer discounts or incentives for using reusable bags, so you can save money while helping the environment.

There are many benefits to using reusable bags. For one, they are more durable than plastic bags, so you can carry heavier items without worrying about the bag tearing. They are also more comfortable to carry, with sturdy handles that won't cut into your hands like thin plastic bags.

Reusable bags are also more versatile than plastic bags. They come in a variety of shapes and sizes, so you can choose the one that best suits your needs. Some are designed for grocery shopping, with insulated compartments for keeping food cold. Others are perfect for carrying books or other items.

Finally, using reusable bags is an excellent way to set an example for others. When you bring your reusable bags to the grocery store, you show others that it's possible to make eco-friendly choices in everyday life. You may even inspire others to make the switch to reusable bags themselves.

In conclusion, using reusable bags instead of plastic bags is a simple but powerful way to reduce your carbon footprint and make more sustainable choices. By choosing to use reusable bags, you can help to reduce pollution, conserve resources, and protect the planet for future generations. So next time you go shopping, don't forget to bring your reusable bag!

Number 26: Use a refillable bottle instead of buying bottled drinks

There is no denying that staying hydrated is essential for leading a healthy and active lifestyle. But, what's the best way to stay hydrated? Is it by buying bottled drinks, or should we opt for a refillable water bottle instead?

The answer is simple - using a refillable water bottle is a far better option than buying bottled drinks. Here are some reasons why:

1. It's eco-friendly

The production of bottled drinks requires a lot of resources, including oil, water, and energy. Furthermore, most water bottles end up in landfills, where they take hundreds of years to decompose. By using a refillable water bottle, you can reduce your carbon footprint and help save the environment.

2. It saves money

Buying bottled drinks can be expensive, especially if you consume them regularly. On the other hand, a refillable water bottle is a one-time investment that can last for years. Furthermore, most public places, such as parks, gyms, and schools, have water fountains where you can refill your bottle for free.

3. It's convenient
Carrying a refillable water bottle with you can be incredibly convenient. You can take it with you wherever you go and refill it whenever you need to. You don't have to worry about running out of water, and you can stay hydrated throughout the day.

4. It's healthier

Bottled drinks often contain added sugars, preservatives, and artificial flavors. On the other hand, water is free of calories and additives, making it the healthiest option for staying hydrated. By using a refillable water bottle, you can ensure that you're consuming only clean and pure water.

In conclusion, using a refillable water bottle is a simple yet effective way to stay hydrated while also helping the environment and saving money. So, the next time you're tempted to buy a bottled drink, consider investing in a refillable water bottle instead. Your wallet, your health, and the planet will thank you.

Number 27: Use a bike/walk instead of driving short distances

It's no secret that cars are a significant contributor to air pollution, but did you know that short car trips are actually the most polluting? Cars emit more pollutants per mile during the first few minutes of operation, as the engine warms up and the catalytic converter begins to work. This means that if you're using your car to make a quick trip to the store or to drop off a package, you're actually doing more harm than good.

On the other hand, walking or cycling not only reduces emissions, but it also has a positive impact on your health. Walking or cycling for short distances can help you burn calories, improve cardiovascular health, and reduce the risk of chronic diseases such as diabetes and heart disease. It's also a great way to get some fresh air and enjoy the outdoors.

Another benefit of walking or cycling is that it can save you money. If you're only traveling a short distance, the cost of gas and wear and tear on your car can add up quickly. By walking or cycling, you can save money on gas, parking, and maintenance costs.

Of course, there are some situations where walking or cycling may not be feasible. If you're carrying heavy items or if the weather is bad, it may be safer and more practical to use a car. However, in many cases, we rely on our cars out of habit or convenience, rather than necessity.

If you're interested in reducing your environmental impact and improving your health, consider making the switch to walking or cycling for short trips. You don't need fancy equipment or special clothing – all you need is a comfortable pair of shoes or a reliable bike. By taking small steps to reduce your carbon footprint, you can make a big difference for the planet and for yourself.

Number 28: Cut down on alcohol consumption

Cutting down on alcohol consumption is a smart move for anyone who wants to improve their health and well-being while saving money. Here are some tips that can help you reduce your alcohol intake:

1. Set realistic goals

It is essential to set realistic goals. For instance, you may decide to reduce your alcohol intake by a specific percentage, such as 50% or 75%, or limit your drinking to specific days of the week. Whatever your goals are, make sure they are achievable and that you are committed to them.

2. Keep track of your drinking

Keeping track of your drinking can help you identify patterns and triggers that lead to excessive alcohol consumption. You can use a journal or an app to record how much you drink, when you drink, and why you drink. This information can help you make informed decisions about your drinking habits and identify areas where you need to make changes.

3. Avoid triggers

Triggers are situations that make you want to drink more, such as social events, stress, or boredom. Avoiding triggers or finding healthy alternatives to cope with them can help you reduce your alcohol intake. For instance, you can engage in physical activity, such as jogging or yoga, to relieve stress or find a hobby that you enjoy to combat boredom.

4. Drink slowly and alternate with water

Drinking slowly and alternating alcoholic drinks with water can help you reduce your alcohol intake and stay hydrated. It can also help you avoid getting drunk quickly and reduce the risk of hangovers.

Moreover, drinking water can help you feel full, reducing the urge to drink more.

5. Seek support

If you find it challenging to cut down on your alcohol consumption, seek support from family members, friends, or a healthcare provider.

In conclusion, cutting down on alcohol consumption is a crucial step towards improving your health and well-being. By setting realistic goals, keeping track of your drinking, avoiding triggers, drinking slowly and alternating with water, and seeking support, you can reduce your alcohol intake and enjoy a healthier and happier life.

Number 29: Use free apps/tools for productivity & organization

As our lives become increasingly digital, we have access to a plethora of free apps and tools that can help us stay productive and organized. Whether you are a student, an entrepreneur, or a busy parent, these tools can help you stay on top of your tasks and manage your time more effectively. In this article, we will explore some of the best free apps and tools for productivity and organization.

1. Trello

Trello is a free project management app that helps you organize and prioritize tasks. You can create boards for different projects and add cards to each board for individual tasks. You can also assign due dates, add comments, and attach files to each card. Trello is a great tool for individuals and teams who need to manage multiple projects simultaneously.

2. Google Drive

Google Drive is a cloud-based storage solution that allows you to store and share files online. You can create documents, spreadsheets, and presentations in Google Drive and share them with others. This tool is especially useful for teams who need to collaborate on documents and projects.

3. Evernote

Evernote is a note-taking app that helps you keep track of your ideas, thoughts, and to-do lists. You can create notes, add tags, and organize them into notebooks. Evernote also has a web clipper extension that allows you to save articles and web pages for later.

4. RescueTime

RescueTime is a time-tracking app that helps you understand how you spend your time. It tracks the time you spend on different websites and applications and provides you with detailed reports. You can use this tool to identify time-wasting activities and improve your productivity.

In conclusion, these free apps and tools can help you stay productive and organized in your personal and professional life. With the help of these tools, you can manage your tasks, stay focused, and improve your productivity. Try out some of these apps and see how they can help you achieve your goals.

Number 30: Cut down on cable or streaming services

In today's world, entertainment has become a significant aspect of our lives. We all love to watch TV shows, movies, and sports events to relieve stress and relax after a long day. However, entertainment services can be expensive, and paying for cable or streaming services every month can put a dent in your budget. The good news is that there are ways to cut down on these services and save money.

Firstly, consider canceling your cable subscription. Cable TV can be expensive, and you may not need all the channels that come with your package. You can opt for a basic package that includes only the channels you watch regularly. Alternatively, you can switch to online streaming services that offer live TV channels at a lower cost. Some popular streaming services for live TV include Hulu Live TV, YouTube TV, and Sling TV.

Another way to save money is by sharing your streaming accounts with family or friends. Most streaming services allow you to create multiple profiles, and you can share the cost of the subscription with others. For example, you can share your Netflix account with your siblings or roommates and split the cost.

Moreover, you can cut down on your streaming services by choosing the ones that offer the content you watch the most. Do you prefer watching movies over TV shows? Then you can opt for a movie-focused streaming service like HBO Max or Amazon Prime Video. Similarly, if you're a sports fan, you can subscribe to a sports-focused streaming service like ESPN+ or DAZN.

Lastly, you can save money by taking advantage of free trials and promotions. Many streaming services offer free trials for a limited period, and you can use this opportunity to binge-watch your favorite shows and movies without paying a dime. Additionally, some services offer discounts and promotions during festive seasons, and you can take advantage of these to save money.

In conclusion, cutting down on cable or streaming services is an excellent way to save money. You can cancel your cable subscription, share your streaming accounts, choose the services that offer the content you watch the most, and take advantage of free trials and promotions. By doing so, you'll be able to enjoy your favorite shows and movies without breaking the bank.

Number 31: Go to the library instead of buying books

Going to the library is free. With the rising costs of books, it can become expensive to build a personal library. By borrowing books from the library, you can save money and still enjoy a wide variety of titles.

Additionally, libraries offer a vast selection of books. From bestsellers to classics, non-fiction to fiction, the library has something for everyone. It's also a great way to discover new authors and genres without committing to buying a book.

Libraries also provide a quiet and peaceful space to read. With comfortable seating, free Wi-Fi, and a relaxed atmosphere, libraries are the perfect place to escape from the distractions of everyday life and immerse yourself in a good book.

Another advantage of borrowing books from the library is that it's eco-friendly. By sharing books rather than buying them, you're reducing your carbon footprint and contributing to a sustainable future.

Lastly, going to the library is a great way to support your local community. Libraries rely on funding and support from their communities to continue providing free services. By using and promoting your local library, you're helping to ensure its survival and the availability of its resources for future generations.

In conclusion, going to the library instead of buying books has numerous benefits. It's free, offers a vast selection of books, provides a quiet and peaceful space to read, is eco-friendly, and supports your local community. So next time you're in the mood for a good book, consider visiting your local library.

Number 32: Buy used cars instead of new ones

In recent years, the trend of buying used cars instead of new ones has gained significant momentum. While the idea of owning a brand new car can be alluring, the reality is that purchasing a used car can be a far more prudent decision. Here are some reasons why:

1. Cost: This is the most obvious advantage of buying a used car. A brand new car loses a significant amount of its value as soon as it is driven off the lot. In contrast, a used car has already undergone this initial depreciation, making it significantly cheaper to purchase. Additionally, insurance rates for used cars tend to be lower than those for new cars.

2. Reliability: Contrary to popular belief, used cars can be just as reliable as new ones. In fact, many used cars have already undergone any necessary repairs and maintenance, making them more dependable than a new car that may need to be brought in for repairs. Additionally, many used cars come with warranties or maintenance plans, giving the buyer added peace of mind.

3. Variety: When buying a used car, the buyer has a much wider selection to choose from. Instead of being limited to the latest models, the buyer can choose from a range of makes, models, and years. This can be especially advantageous for those on a tight budget, as they can find a car that meets their needs at a much lower price point.

4. Environmental impact: Buying a used car is a more environmentally-friendly option than buying a new one. The production of new cars requires a significant amount of energy and resources, and the disposal of old cars can also be an environmental

hazard. By purchasing a used car, the buyer is helping to reduce the demand for new cars, which in turn reduces the amount of energy and resources needed to produce them.

Overall, there are many compelling reasons to consider buying a used car instead of a new one. From the lower cost to the wider selection, the advantages are clear. Of course, it is important to do your research and take the time to find a car that meets your needs and fits your budget. With a little patience and diligence, you can find a used car that will serve you well for years to come.

Number 33: Cut down on eating fast food

Fast food is a popular option for people who are always on the go. It is quick, convenient, and affordable. However, consuming fast food regularly can have serious negative health consequences. Fast food is high in calories, unhealthy fats, sugars, and sodium, which can increase the risk of obesity, diabetes, heart disease, and other health problems. Cutting down on eating fast food can improve overall health and well-being.

The first step to cutting down on fast food is to plan ahead. When you are busy and on the go, it can be easy to opt for fast food. However, if you make a plan, you can avoid the temptation. You can pack healthy snacks and meals to take with you when you are out and about. This will ensure that you always have healthy options available.

Another way to cut down on eating fast food is to cook at home. Cooking at home allows you to control the ingredients and the portion sizes. You can make healthier versions of your favorite fast food meals at home. For example, you can make a homemade burger with lean ground beef, whole-grain buns, and fresh vegetables. This will be much healthier than a burger from a fast food restaurant.

If you do decide to eat out, choose healthier options. Many fast food restaurants now offer healthier options on their menus. Look for items that are low in calories, saturated fat, and sodium. You can also ask for modifications to make your meal healthier. For example, you can ask for a salad instead of fries or a grilled chicken sandwich instead of a burger.

Finally, be mindful of your portion sizes. Fast food restaurants often serve large portions, which can lead to overeating. If you do decide to eat fast food, choose smaller portions or share a meal with a friend.

In conclusion, cutting down on eating fast food is important for overall health and well-being. By planning ahead, cooking at home, choosing healthier options when eating out, and being mindful of portion sizes, you can reduce your consumption of fast food and improve your health while spending less. Remember that small changes can lead to big results.

Number 34: Use a rain barrel to collect water for gardening

If you are a gardener, you know the importance of water for your plants. But with water becoming an increasingly scarce resource, it's important to find ways to conserve and reuse it. One way to do this is by using a rain barrel to collect rainwater.

A rain barrel is a container that collects rainwater from your roof using a downspout. It's a simple and effective way to collect water that would otherwise go to waste. The collected water can then be used for watering your garden, washing your car, or other outdoor activities.

There are many benefits to using a rain barrel for gardening. Firstly, it's an eco-friendly way to water your plants, as it reduces the amount of water you use from the municipal supply. This can help you save money on your water bill, too. Secondly, rainwater is naturally free of chlorine and other chemicals that are often found in tap water. This makes it a healthier option for your plants. Finally, using a rain barrel can help reduce water runoff, which can be a problem during heavy rains. By collecting rainwater, you can help prevent soil erosion and other environmental problems.

Setting up a rain barrel is easy. You will need a barrel, a downspout diverter, and a few basic tools. You can buy a rain barrel at your local hardware store or online. Make sure to choose a barrel that is made of food-grade plastic and has a tight-fitting lid to prevent insects and debris from getting in.

Next, you'll need to install a downspout diverter. This is a device that connects your downspout to your rain barrel. It allows rainwater to flow into the barrel, but also prevents overflow during heavy rains. You can buy a downspout diverter at your local hardware store or online.

Once you've installed your rain barrel, it's important to maintain it properly. Clean it out regularly to prevent algae and other contaminants from building up. You can also add a screen to the top of the barrel to keep out debris and insects.

Using a rain barrel to collect water for gardening is a simple and effective way to conserve water and protect the environment. It's an easy DIY project that can be done in just a few hours, and it can save you money in the long run. So why not give it a try?

Number 35: Use a programmable coffee maker

For many of us, coffee is an essential part of our daily routine. Whether you are a busy professional, a student, or a stay-at-home parent, a cup of coffee can help you start your day off right and keep you energized throughout the day. However, buying coffee from a coffee shop or café can be expensive, especially if you are a regular coffee drinker. Fortunately, there is a simple solution to this problem – using a programmable coffee maker.

A programmable coffee maker is a great investment for anyone who wants to save money on their coffee expenses. These machines allow you to set the time for your coffee to start brewing, so you can wake up to a fresh cup of coffee every morning without having to spend money at a café. This is especially useful for people who have busy schedules and don't have time to wait in line for coffee.

In addition to saving money on your daily coffee expenses, a programmable coffee maker can also help you save money in the long run. Instead of buying expensive coffee pods or capsules, you can use regular ground coffee beans, which are much cheaper. This will help you save money on your coffee expenses over time, without sacrificing the quality of your coffee.

Another benefit of using a programmable coffee maker is that it allows you to control the amount of coffee you make. This means you can make just the right amount of coffee you need, without wasting any coffee or money. You can also adjust the strength of your coffee to your liking, which is not always possible with pre-made coffee from a café.

Finally, a programmable coffee maker can help you save time and energy in the morning. Instead of spending time waiting in line at a café or making coffee manually, you can simply set your coffee maker to start brewing at a specific time. This will allow you to focus on other things in the morning, such as getting ready for work or getting your kids ready for school.

In conclusion, using a programmable coffee maker is a great way to save money on your daily coffee expenses. With this machine, you can wake up to a fresh cup of coffee every morning without having to spend money at a café. You can also save money in the long run by using regular ground coffee beans instead of expensive coffee pods or capsules. Additionally, a programmable coffee maker can help you save time and energy in the morning, allowing you to focus on other things. So, if you're a regular coffee drinker looking to save money and time, consider investing in a programmable coffee maker today.

Number 36: Cut down on personal care expenses

1. Simplify your routine

One of the easiest ways to save money on beauty and personal care products is to simplify your routine. Do you really need five different serums for your face or five different shampoos for your hair? Probably not. Instead, pare down your routine to the essentials: a gentle cleanser, a moisturizer, and a sunscreen for your face, and a basic shampoo and conditioner for your hair. This will not only save you money, but it will also save you time and energy.

2. Buy multipurpose products

Another way to save money on beauty and personal care products is to look for multipurpose products that can serve multiple functions. For example, a tinted moisturizer can act as both a moisturizer and a foundation, or a lip and cheek tint can be used for both your lips and cheeks. By investing in multipurpose products, you can cut down on the number of products you need to buy, which will save you money in the long run.

3. Look for sales and discounts

One of the easiest ways to save money on beauty and personal care products is to look for sales and discounts. Many retailers offer regular sales, promotions, and discounts on their products, so keep an eye out for these deals. You can also sign up for email lists and loyalty programs to receive exclusive discounts and offers.

4. DIY your own products

Another way to save money on beauty and personal care products is to DIY your own products. Many beauty and personal care products can be made at home using natural ingredients like coconut oil, honey, and avocado. By making your own products, you can save money and ensure that you're using natural, non-toxic ingredients on your skin and hair.

5. Use coupons and cashback apps

Finally, you can save money on beauty and personal care products by using coupons and cashback apps.

In conclusion, there are many ways to cut down on beauty and personal care expenses without sacrificing your appearance. By simplifying your routine, buying multipurpose products, looking for sales and discounts, DIYing your own products, and using coupons and cashback apps, you can save money and still look and feel great.

Number 37: Use a crockpot to cook instead of the oven

Using a crockpot to cook instead of the oven is a great way to save time and energy. Crockpots are also known as slow cookers, and they are an excellent option for busy families or those who want to make meals ahead of time. Crockpots can cook a variety of dishes, from stews and soups to roasts and casseroles. They are also great for cooking meals that require low and slow cooking.

One of the biggest advantages of using a crockpot is that it uses less energy than an oven. Crockpots are designed to cook at a low temperature for a long time, which means that they use a fraction of the energy that an oven would use. This is especially important for those who are trying to save money on their energy bills.

Using a crockpot is also a great way to make meals ahead of time. Many people use their crockpots to cook meals on the weekend and then reheat them throughout the week. This is a great way to save time during the week and to ensure that you always have a healthy meal on hand.

Another advantage of using a crockpot is that it is a very hands-off cooking method. Once you have added your ingredients to the crockpot, you can leave it to cook for several hours without having to check on it. This means that you can go about your day without having to worry about your meal.

Crockpots are also great for cooking tough cuts of meat. When you cook meat in a crockpot, it becomes incredibly tender and juicy. This is because the low and slow cooking method allows the meat to break down slowly, resulting in a delicious and tender meal.

Overall, using a crockpot to cook instead of the oven is a great option for those who want to save time and energy. Crockpots are a great way to make meals ahead of time, and they are perfect for cooking meals that require low and slow cooking.

Number 38: Use a reusable razor instead of disposable ones

Disposable razors are a common item found in many households, but they are also a significant contributor to the world's waste problem. According to a study by the Environmental Protection Agency, over two billion disposable razors are thrown away each year in the United States alone. These razors end up in landfills or in our oceans, where they can take hundreds of years to decompose.

In contrast, a reusable razor can last for years with proper care and maintenance. These razors are typically made of metal or durable plastic and can be used multiple times before needing to be replaced. While they may be more expensive upfront than disposable razors, they can ultimately save you money in the long run and reduce your environmental impact.

Using a reusable razor is also a more sustainable option because it eliminates the need for disposable packaging. Disposable razors often come in plastic packaging that is not recyclable, which only adds to the amount of waste we produce. Reusable razors typically come in minimal or recyclable packaging, which reduces the overall amount of waste.

Another benefit of using a reusable razor is that they can provide a closer shave. Disposable razors are often made with lower-quality blades, which can lead to razor burn, cuts, and irritation. Reusable razors typically have higher-quality blades that can provide a smoother and closer shave.

When it comes to choosing a reusable razor, there are several options to consider. Safety razors are a popular choice, as they are easy to use and typically have interchangeable blades. Straight razors are also an option, but require more skill and practice to use safely. There are also electric razors, which can be used multiple times and don't require replacement blades.

In conclusion, using a reusable razor is a simple and effective way to reduce your environmental impact and save money in the long run.

Number 39: Use a space heater instead of heating the entire house

As the temperatures drop, many homeowners are looking for ways to save money on their heating bills. One option that is becoming increasingly popular is to use a space heater instead of heating the entire house. While this may seem like a simple solution, there are several factors to consider before making the switch.

First, it is important to understand how space heaters work. Unlike central heating systems that heat the entire house, space heaters use electricity or gas to heat a small area. This means that you can turn off your central heating system and only heat the rooms that you are using. This can be a great way to save money on your heating bill, as you are only using energy to heat the rooms you are actually using.

However, there are some drawbacks to using a space heater. One of the biggest concerns is safety. Space heaters can be a fire hazard if they are not used properly. It is important to keep them away from flammable materials, such as curtains and furniture, and to never leave them unattended. Additionally, it is important to choose a space heater that has safety features, such as a tip-over switch that automatically turns off the heater if it is knocked over.

Another concern with using a space heater is energy efficiency. While it may seem like you are saving money by only heating one room, space heaters can be very energy-intensive. This means that you may end up using more energy than you would if you were heating the entire house. Additionally, if you have an older home with poor insulation, you may find that the heat generated by the space heater quickly escapes through cracks and gaps in your home's structure.

Despite these concerns, there are some situations where using a space heater can be a good choice. For example, if you only use one or two rooms in your home, such as a home office or a bedroom, a space heater can be a cost-effective way to heat those rooms. Additionally, if you live in a small apartment or condo, a space heater can be a good choice for heating your living space.

In conclusion, using a space heater instead of heating the entire house can be a good way to save money on your heating bill. However, it is important to consider safety and energy efficiency before making the switch. If you do decide to use a space heater, be sure to choose a model with safety features and to use it properly to avoid any fire hazards. Additionally, be aware that space heaters can be energy-intensive, so it may not be the best choice for all situations.

Number 40: Cut down on unnecessary travel expenses

As the saying goes, "money doesn't grow on trees," and in today's economy, it's more important than ever to cut back on unnecessary expenses. One area where many people overspend is on travel, whether it's for vacations or other leisure activities. However, with a few simple strategies, it's possible to reduce these costs and enjoy more affordable travel.

One way to cut down on expenses is to plan ahead. This means researching various travel options, comparing prices, and booking early. Many airlines, hotels, and other travel providers offer discounts for early bookings, which can save you a significant amount of money. Additionally, you can use online tools such as travel comparison sites to find the best deals and save on travel expenses.

Another way to save money on travel is to be flexible with your travel dates. Traveling during peak seasons or on weekends can be more expensive, so consider traveling during off-peak times or on weekdays. Additionally, you can explore alternative destinations that may offer lower prices or better deals. For example, instead of traveling to a popular tourist destination, you can opt for a nearby city or town that is less well-known but still offers plenty of attractions and activities.

When it comes to accommodations, there are many ways to save money as well. Instead of staying in a high-end hotel, you can consider alternative options such as hostels, vacation rentals, or camping. These options can be significantly cheaper, and they also offer unique experiences that you may not find in a traditional hotel. Additionally, you can look for hotels that offer free breakfast or other amenities that can help you save money on meals and other expenses.

Finally, it's important to be mindful of your spending when you're traveling. This means avoiding unnecessary expenses such as eating out at expensive restaurants or buying souvenirs that you don't need. Instead, you can bring your own food or snacks, explore local markets and street food vendors, and find free or low-cost activities and attractions.

In conclusion, cutting down on unnecessary travel expenses is a smart way to save money and enjoy more affordable travel. By planning ahead, being flexible, exploring alternative options, and being mindful of your spending, you can reduce your travel costs without sacrificing the quality of your experience.

Number 41: Use a clothes steamer instead of dry cleaning

Dry cleaning not only costs a lot of money but it is also harmful to the environment.

Fortunately, there is an alternative to dry cleaning that is not only environmentally friendly but also saves money: using a clothes steamer. Clothes steamers are a great alternative to dry cleaning because they use steam to remove wrinkles, odors, and stains from clothes.

Using a clothes steamer is simple and easy. First, hang your clothes on a hanger and then fill the steamer with water. Once the water is heated, the steam is released, and you can use it to remove wrinkles and odors from your clothes. Clothes steamers are effective for most types of fabrics, including delicate fabrics that cannot be dry cleaned.

One of the benefits of using a clothes steamer is that it is a one-time investment that can last for years. In contrast, dry cleaning can cost a lot of money and becomes an ongoing expense. Moreover, dry cleaning uses chemicals such as perchloroethylene, which is harmful to the environment and can cause health problems.

Using a clothes steamer is a great way to reduce your carbon footprint. Clothes steamers use less water than a washing machine and do not use harsh chemicals that can pollute the environment. Additionally, clothes steamers use less energy than dry cleaning machines, which means you are reducing your carbon footprint in multiple ways.

Another benefit of using a clothes steamer is that it is gentle on your clothes. Dry cleaning can cause damage to your clothes over time, but using a clothes steamer is gentle and won't cause any damage to the fabric. Clothes steamers are also great for removing stains and odors from clothes, which means you can avoid having to buy new clothes because of a stain or odor.

In conclusion, using a clothes steamer instead of dry cleaning is a great way to save money and reduce your carbon footprint. Clothes steamers are easy to use, effective, and gentle on your clothes. By making a small investment in a clothes steamer, you can save money in the long run and do your part in reducing your impact on the environment.

Number 42: Cut down on gift expenses by making homemade gifts

Making your own gifts is a creative and thoughtful way to show your loved ones how much you care, without breaking the bank. Here are some tips and ideas for making homemade gifts this holiday season:

1. Start with a plan

Before you begin making gifts, create a list of everyone you want to give gifts to and brainstorm ideas for each person. Consider their interests and hobbies, as well as your own skills and resources.

2. Use what you have

You don't need to spend a lot of money on supplies for homemade gifts. Look around your home and see what you already have on hand. For example, if you have a stash of fabric, you could make a quilt or a set of reusable cloth napkins.

3. Get creative with packaging

Presentation is key when it comes to gift-giving, and you can make your homemade gifts stand out with creative packaging. Use recycled materials, such as newspaper or brown paper bags, to wrap gifts and add a homemade touch with ribbon or twine.

4. Make edible gifts

Food is always a crowd-pleaser, and homemade treats are a thoughtful way to show you care. Consider baking cookies, making homemade jams or chutneys, or creating a personalized spice blend.

5. DIY beauty products

You can also create your own beauty products, such as bath bombs, lip balms, or body scrubs. These are easy to make with simple ingredients, and you can customize them with your favorite scents and colors.

In conclusion, homemade gifts are a thoughtful and budget-friendly way to show your loved ones how much you care. With a little creativity and planning, you can make this holiday season special without breaking the bank.

Number 43: Use a reusable menstrual cup instead of disposables

The menstrual cycle is a natural process that occurs in the female body every month. While menstruation is a normal occurrence, the products used to manage it are not always eco-friendly. Disposable pads and tampons are the most commonly used menstrual products, but they have a significant impact on the environment. They are made from plastic and other synthetic materials that do not decompose. They end up in landfills and take hundreds of years to break down, causing harm to the environment. A reusable menstrual cup is a sustainable alternative that can help reduce waste and save the environment.

Reusable menstrual cups are made from medical-grade silicone or latex rubber and are designed to be inserted into the vagina. They are reusable and can last for up to ten years with proper care. Unlike disposable pads and tampons, menstrual cups do not absorb menstrual fluid. Instead, they collect it, making them an ideal option for those who have heavy periods. They are also leak-proof, easy to use, and comfortable to wear.

When it comes to the environment, reusable menstrual cups are a much better option than disposable products. They produce zero waste, unlike disposable products that generate tons of waste every year. In addition, menstrual cups do not contain any harmful chemicals, making them safe for the environment and the body. They are also cost-effective in the long run, as they can be used for years, reducing the need to purchase disposable products every month.

Using a reusable menstrual cup is not only good for the environment but also for your health. Disposable menstrual products contain harmful chemicals that can cause irritation and infections. Reusable menstrual cups are made from medical-grade materials and do not contain any chemicals, making them safe for the body.

In conclusion, using a reusable menstrual cup is an eco-friendly and cost-effective option that can help reduce waste and protect the environment. It is a sustainable alternative to disposable menstrual products that are harmful to the environment and the body. By making the switch to a reusable menstrual cup, you can help reduce waste and save the environment. It is a small step that can make a big difference in the long run.

Number 44: Use a reusable shopping bag instead of disposable bags

Disposable plastic bags are a major source of pollution and waste. They are made from non-renewable resources such as oil and gas, and take hundreds of years to decompose. They also pose a threat to wildlife, as animals can mistake them for food and ingest them, leading to injury or death.

On the other hand, reusable shopping bags are made from durable materials such as canvas, jute, or recycled plastic. They can be used over and over again, reducing the need for disposable bags. Some reusable bags even come with a lifetime guarantee, so you can use them for years without needing to buy a new one.

Using a reusable shopping bag can also save you money in the long run. While a single-use plastic bag may only cost a few cents, over time these costs add up. In some areas, retailers even charge a fee for disposable bags, which can add up to a significant amount over time.

By contrast, a reusable shopping bag can be used for years, making it a cost-effective alternative to disposable bags. Some stores even offer discounts or incentives for customers who bring their own bags.

In addition to saving money, using a reusable shopping bag can also help you stay organized and efficient when shopping. Many reusable bags have multiple compartments and pockets, making them ideal for carrying groceries and other items. They can also be folded up and stored easily, taking up less space in your car or home.

Overall, there are many benefits to using a reusable shopping bag instead of disposable bags. By reducing waste, conserving resources, and saving money, you can make a positive impact on the environment while simplifying your shopping routine.

Number 45: Cut down on home decor expenses with DIY projects

Home decor is as important as any other part of our lives, but it can get expensive. With the current economic climate, everyone is looking for ways to cut down on their expenses. One way to do that is by indulging in Do-It-Yourself (DIY) projects for home decor. Not only do you save money, but you also get to personalize your home with unique pieces that reflect your personality.

DIY projects for home decor are becoming increasingly popular as people realize that they can create beautiful pieces for their homes with minimal effort and at a fraction of the cost of buying them from a store. Here are some ways you can cut down on home decor expenses with DIY projects.

1. Repurpose old items

One of the easiest ways to save money on home decor is by repurposing old items. For example, an old ladder can be transformed into a bookshelf, a coffee table, or a plant stand. An old dresser can be painted and used as a TV stand or a storage unit. The possibilities are endless, and all it takes is a little creativity and elbow grease.

2. Use inexpensive materials

Another way to save money on home decor is by using inexpensive materials. For example, You can use fabric to make throw pillows or curtains, or use wallpaper to create an accent wall.

3. Learn new skills

Learning new skills can also help you save money on home decor. For example, if you learn how to sew, you can make your own curtains, tablecloths, and even bedding. If you learn how to paint, you can create your own artwork for your home.

4. Plan your projects

Planning your DIY projects can also help you save money. Instead of starting a project without a plan, take the time to research and plan out each step.

In conclusion, home decor doesn't have to be expensive. With DIY projects, you can create beautiful pieces for your home while saving money. Repurposing old items, using inexpensive materials, learning new skills, shopping secondhand, and planning your projects are all great ways to cut down on home decor expenses.

Number 46: Use a low-flow showerhead to save on water bills

Water conservation has become a pressing issue in today's world, and one of the simplest ways to save water is by using a low-flow showerhead. A low-flow showerhead is designed to reduce the amount of water that flows through it, which in turn reduces the amount of water we use while showering. Not only does it help to conserve water, but it also helps to lower your water bills.

Low-flow showerheads use less water than traditional showerheads by restricting the flow of water through the showerhead's nozzle. They come in different designs, but they all work on the same principle of reducing the amount of water that comes out of the showerhead. Low-flow showerheads typically use less than 2.5 gallons of water per minute, which is significantly less than the 5-8 gallons per minute that traditional showerheads can use.

Using a low-flow showerhead can save you a significant amount of money on your water bills. According to the Environmental Protection Agency (EPA), an average family of four can save up to 2,900 gallons of water per year by switching to a low-flow showerhead. This translates to savings of up to $70 per year on your water bill.

In addition to saving you money, using a low-flow showerhead also helps to conserve water. Water is a finite resource, and with the world's population increasing rapidly, it has become more important than ever to conserve water. By using a low-flow showerhead, you can do your part to conserve water and reduce your carbon footprint.

Installing a low-flow showerhead is easy and can be done by anyone. Most low-flow showerheads come with installation instructions, and all you need is a wrench and some plumber's tape. Simply unscrew your old showerhead and replace it with the new low-flow showerhead. It should take no more than 10 minutes to install.

In conclusion, using a low-flow showerhead is an easy and effective way to save water and reduce your water bills. It's a simple change that can have a significant impact on the environment and your wallet. So, if you haven't already, consider making the switch to a low-flow showerhead today.

Number 47: Cut down on impulse purchases

Impulse purchases can quickly add up and leave you with an empty wallet and a closet full of things you may not even need or want. If you're looking to cut down on impulse purchases, there are some strategies you can try that will help you stay on track and only buy the things you really want or need.

First, it's important to identify your triggers. When are you most likely to make an impulse purchase? Is it when you're stressed, bored, or shopping with friends? Once you know your triggers, you can start to develop strategies to overcome them. For example, if you find yourself making impulse purchases when you're bored, try finding other activities to occupy your time, such as going for a walk or reading a book.

Another strategy is to create a budget and stick to it. This means setting aside a specific amount of money each month for discretionary spending, and not going over that amount. You can also try using cash instead of credit cards, as it's easier to keep track of how much you're spending when you're using physical money.

It's also helpful to give yourself time before making a purchase. If you see something you really want, wait a day or two before making the purchase. This will give you time to think about whether or not you really need or want the item, and if it's worth the money you'll be spending on it.

Another way to cut down on impulse purchases is to unsubscribe from marketing emails and unfollow social media accounts that promote products. This will help you avoid temptation and reduce the number of ads and promotions you see on a daily basis.

Finally, it's important to remember that you don't need to buy something just because it's on sale or because everyone else has it. It's okay to say no and only buy the things that you truly want or need.

In conclusion, cutting down on impulse purchases requires discipline and self-awareness. By identifying your triggers, setting a budget, giving yourself time before making a purchase, and avoiding temptation, you can develop healthy spending habits and save money in the long run.

Number 48: Use a reusable lunch container instead of disposable

The concept of using a reusable lunch container is simple yet effective. Instead of buying a new container every time you have to pack your lunch, you can use a container that can be washed and reused multiple times. This not only saves money but also reduces the amount of waste generated. According to a study, the average person generates around 4.4 pounds of waste per day, and a significant portion of this waste is from disposable products like lunch containers.

Using a reusable lunch container can save you money in several ways. Firstly, you don't have to buy a new container every time you pack your lunch. This may not seem like a significant expense, but over time, it adds up. Secondly, using a reusable container also means that you can buy your food in bulk, which is usually cheaper than buying individual portions. By buying in bulk, you can save money on the cost per serving, and you can also avoid the extra packaging that comes with individual servings. Thirdly, using a reusable container can also help you save money by motivating you to prepare your meals at home instead of eating out. Eating out can be expensive, and by packing your lunch, you can save a significant amount of money every week.

Apart from saving money, using a reusable lunch container is also environmentally friendly. Disposable lunch containers are usually made of plastic, which is non-biodegradable and takes hundreds of years to decompose. As a result, they end up in landfills or oceans, polluting the environment and harming wildlife. By using a reusable container, you can reduce the amount of plastic waste generated and help protect the environment.

In conclusion, using a reusable lunch container is not only a cost-effective solution but also an eco-friendly one. It can help you save money by reducing the need to buy new containers, buying food in bulk, and motivating you to prepare your meals at home. At the same time, it can also help reduce the amount of plastic waste generated and protect the environment. So, the next time you pack your lunch, consider using a reusable container instead of a disposable one.

Number 49: Use a refillable ink cartridge instead of buying new

When it comes to printing documents or photos, ink cartridges are essential. However, over time, ink cartridges can become expensive and wasteful. Fortunately, there is an alternative: using a refillable ink cartridge.

A refillable ink cartridge is exactly what it sounds like - a cartridge that can be refilled with ink instead of being disposed of after it runs out. These cartridges are designed to be used multiple times and can save you money in the long run.

One of the most significant benefits of using a refillable ink cartridge is cost savings. While a new cartridge can cost anywhere from $20 to $60, depending on the brand and model, a refillable cartridge can be refilled for a fraction of the cost. Refilling a cartridge can cost as little as a few dollars, depending on the type of ink you use.

Another benefit of using a refillable ink cartridge is reduced waste. Every year, millions of ink cartridges end up in landfills, where they can take hundreds of years to decompose. By using a refillable cartridge, you can help reduce the amount of waste that ends up in landfills. This is not only better for the environment, but it can also help reduce your carbon footprint.

Using a refillable ink cartridge is also more convenient than buying new cartridges. Instead of having to go to the store every time you run out of ink, you can simply refill the cartridge yourself. This can save you time and money, as well as reduce your carbon footprint.

However, there are some downsides to using a refillable ink cartridge. For example, refilling a cartridge can be messy and time-consuming, especially if you're not familiar with the process. Additionally, some printers may not recognize or accept refilled cartridges, which can cause issues with print quality or even damage the printer.

Despite these downsides, using a refillable ink cartridge is a great way to save money and reduce waste. If you're interested in using a refillable ink cartridge, there are many options available online and in stores. Just be sure to follow the manufacturer's instructions carefully to ensure that you get the best results possible.

Number 50: Cut down on subscription services

Subscription services are becoming increasingly popular in today's digital age. From streaming services like Netflix and Spotify to meal delivery services like Blue Apron and HelloFresh, there seems to be a subscription for everything. While these services may seem convenient and affordable at first, they can quickly add up and become a financial burden. Cutting down on subscription services is a great way to save money and prioritize your spending.

1. Identify which subscriptions you can live without

The first step in cutting down on subscription services is to identify which ones you can live without. Take a look at your bank statements and make a list of all the subscriptions you are currently paying for. Be honest with yourself and ask if you really need each service. If you find yourself not using a particular service or using it very rarely, consider canceling it.

2. Prioritize your subscriptions

Once you have identified the subscriptions you can live without, prioritize the ones that are most important to you. For example, if you use Netflix every day but only use your gym membership once a month, consider canceling the gym membership and keeping the Netflix subscription. Prioritizing your subscriptions will help you save money while still enjoying the services that are most important to you.

3. Look for free alternatives

Many subscription services have free alternatives that offer similar features. For example, instead of paying for a meal delivery service, consider meal planning and cooking at home. Instead of paying for a music streaming service, consider listening to free music on YouTube or Pandora. Finding free alternatives can help you save money and still enjoy the services you love.

4. Set a budget for subscription services

Lastly, set a budget for subscription services. Determine how much you are willing to spend each month on subscriptions and stick to it. This will help you prioritize your spending and avoid overspending on unnecessary services.

In conclusion, cutting down on subscription services is a great way to save money and prioritize your spending. Identify which subscriptions you can live without, prioritize the ones that are most important to you, share subscriptions with family or friends, look for free alternatives, and set a budget for subscription services. By following these steps, you can enjoy the services you love while still saving money.

Number 51: Use a bidet instead of buying toilet paper

The use of bidets is becoming more common around the world. Bidets are popular in many countries, especially in Asia and Europe, as an alternative to toilet paper. Bidets are highly effective and environmentally friendly, and they can help to save money in the long run.

Bidets are devices that are used to clean the genital and anal areas after using the toilet. They are usually placed next to the toilet and consist of a water jet that is directed towards the user. The water jet can be adjusted to suit the user's needs and preferences.

Using a bidet instead of toilet paper has many benefits. Firstly, bidets are more hygienic than toilet paper. They help to remove more bacteria and germs from the skin, which can help to prevent infections and other health problems. Bidets also help to reduce the risk of skin irritation and other problems that can be caused by using toilet paper.

Another benefit of using a bidet is that it is more environmentally friendly than using toilet paper. Toilet paper is made from trees, which means that it contributes to deforestation and other environmental problems. Bidets, on the other hand, use water, which is a renewable resource. By using a bidet instead of toilet paper, you can help to reduce your carbon footprint and protect the environment.

Using a bidet can also help you to save money in the long run. Although bidets may be more expensive to purchase and install than toilet paper, they are more cost-effective in the long run. You will no longer need to buy toilet paper, which can be a significant expense over time. Instead, you can use water, which is much cheaper and more sustainable.

In conclusion, using a bidet instead of toilet paper is a great way to save money and reduce waste. Bidets are more hygienic, environmentally friendly, and cost-effective than using toilet paper. If you are looking for a way to improve your hygiene and reduce your environmental impact, consider installing a bidet in your bathroom.

Number 52: Cut down on hair salon expenses by cutting it at home

Hair is an essential part of our appearance, and we all want to have it well-groomed and presentable. However, frequent visits to the hair salon can be costly, especially if you have long hair or require frequent touch-ups. One way to reduce these expenses is by cutting your hair at home.

Cutting your hair at home may seem daunting at first, but with the right tools and techniques, it can be a simple and effective solution. Here are some tips to help you get started:

Invest in quality tools: To cut your hair at home, you will need a few basic tools, such as a pair of scissors, hair clippers, a comb, and a mirror. It is essential to invest in good quality tools to ensure that you achieve the desired results.

Watch tutorial videos: There are many tutorial videos available online that can teach you how to cut hair at home. These videos can guide you through the entire process, from sectioning your hair to trimming the ends.

Start with small cuts: If you are new to cutting hair, it is best to start with small cuts. Begin by trimming the ends of your hair and gradually work your way up to more significant cuts.

Take your time: Cutting hair at home requires patience and attention to detail. Take your time and make sure that you are cutting your hair evenly and at the right angle.

Ask for help: If you are unsure about cutting your hair, ask a family member or friend to help you. Having a second pair of eyes can make the process easier and ensure that you achieve the desired results.

Cutting your hair at home can save you a significant amount of money in the long run. However, it is essential to remember that cutting your hair is not for everyone. If you are not comfortable with cutting your hair, it is best to leave it to the professionals.

In conclusion, cutting your hair at home is an excellent way to reduce hair salon expenses. With the right tools and techniques, you can achieve professional-looking results from the comfort of your home. Remember to take your time, start with small cuts, and ask for help if needed. Happy cutting!

Number 53: Use a reusable cloth diaper instead of disposables

One of the most significant advantages of using reusable cloth diapers is the positive impact on the environment. Disposable diapers are a significant contributor to the world's landfill waste, with over 20 billion disposable diapers ending up in landfills each year in the United States alone. These diapers can take up to 500 years to decompose, and during this time, they release harmful chemicals and greenhouse gases into the environment. By using cloth diapers, parents can significantly reduce their carbon footprint and contribute to a cleaner and greener world.

Reusable cloth diapers are also more cost-effective in the long run. Although the initial investment in cloth diapers may seem higher than buying disposable diapers, in the long run, it can save parents thousands of dollars. Disposable diapers are used and thrown away after a single use, while cloth diapers can be washed and reused multiple times. Therefore, parents can save money by investing in cloth diapers, which can last for years and can be used for multiple children.

Cloth diapers also offer several benefits to babies. Disposable diapers contain chemicals and synthetic materials that can cause skin irritation and rashes, while cloth diapers are made of natural and breathable materials that are gentle on the baby's skin. Reusable diapers also offer better ventilation, preventing diaper rash and other skin problems. Cloth diapers are also more comfortable for babies and offer better absorption and leakage protection, ensuring that babies stay dry and comfortable for longer periods.

Using cloth diapers also offers a more convenient and hassle-free experience for parents. With disposable diapers, parents have to frequently go to the store to purchase new packs of diapers, while with cloth diapers, they can wash and reuse them as needed. Cloth diapers are also lightweight and easy to carry, making them an ideal option for parents who are always on the go.

In conclusion, using reusable cloth diapers instead of disposable diapers offers several benefits to parents, babies, and the environment. The initial investment may seem higher, but in the long run, it saves money, is more comfortable for babies, and contributes to a cleaner and greener world. So, if you are a parent looking for a sustainable and cost-effective diapering option, consider switching to reusable cloth diapers.

Number 54: Use cloth napkins instead of disposables

Americans use approximately 13 billion pounds of paper towels each year, which equates to 40 pounds per person. The production and disposal of these paper towels contribute to deforestation, water pollution, and waste in landfills. The good news is that there is a simple solution to this problem: using reusable cloth napkins.

Using reusable cloth napkins is an eco-friendly alternative to paper towels and disposable napkins. They come in various sizes, colors, and materials, making them versatile and fashionable for any occasion. They are also durable and can last for years, saving you money in the long run. Cloth napkins are easy to clean, and they can be washed with your regular laundry.

The benefits of using reusable cloth napkins go beyond the environment and your wallet. They also add elegance and class to your dining experience. Cloth napkins provide a sense of sophistication to any occasion, whether it's a fancy dinner party or a casual family meal. They add a touch of luxury to the dining table and make your guests feel special.

Using cloth napkins is also an excellent way to teach your children about sustainability and the importance of reducing waste. By using cloth napkins, you are setting an example for your children to follow. You can also involve them in the process of choosing and washing the napkins, making it a fun and educational activity.

In conclusion, using reusable cloth napkins is a small but powerful step towards a greener and more sustainable future. By making this simple switch in your daily routine, you can reduce waste, save money, and add elegance to your dining experience. It's time to say goodbye to disposable napkins and hello to reusable cloth napkins.

Number 55: Cut down on pet expenses

As pet owners, we all want to provide the best possible care for our furry friends. However, owning a pet can be expensive, especially when it comes to feeding them. The cost of pet food can quickly add up, especially if you have a large pet or multiple pets. Fortunately, there are ways to cut down on pet expenses without compromising on the quality of your pet's diet. One such way is by buying in bulk or making homemade pet food.

Buying in bulk is a great way to save money on pet food. Many pet stores offer bulk discounts on pet food, especially if you buy large bags or cans of food. You can also find great deals on pet food online, especially if you buy in bulk. When buying in bulk, make sure to check the expiration dates on the food to ensure that it won't expire before you can use it all.

Another way to save money on pet food is by making your own homemade pet food. Making your own pet food is not only cost-effective, but it also allows you to control the quality of the ingredients that go into your pet's diet. Homemade pet food can be made from a variety of ingredients such as chicken, rice, sweet potatoes, and vegetables. There are many recipes available online that are easy to follow and use simple ingredients.

When making homemade pet food, it's important to ensure that your pet is getting all the necessary nutrients that they need. It's also important to avoid ingredients that can be harmful to your pet such as onions, garlic, and chocolate. You should also consult with your veterinarian to ensure that your homemade pet food is appropriate for your pet's specific needs.

In addition to buying in bulk and making homemade pet food, there are other ways to save money on pet expenses. For example, you can buy pet supplies in bulk, such as litter or toys. You can also save money by grooming your pet at home instead of taking them to a professional groomer.

In conclusion, owning a pet doesn't have to be expensive. By buying in bulk or making homemade pet food, you can save money on pet expenses without compromising on the quality of your pet's diet.

Remember to always consult with your veterinarian before making any changes to your pet's diet. With a little bit of effort, you can provide your pet with the care they deserve without breaking the bank.

Number 56: Use a reusable food container instead of disposable ones

Using a reusable food container instead of disposable ones is a small but impactful step towards reducing waste and protecting the environment. Single-use plastics, including disposable food containers, are a significant contributor to pollution and environmental degradation. By opting for reusable containers, we can reduce our carbon footprint and help to preserve natural resources.

Disposable food containers are often made from materials such as plastic, styrofoam, or paper, which can take decades or even centuries to decompose. These materials not only take up space in landfills but also pose a threat to wildlife and ecosystems. In addition, the production of disposable containers requires the use of energy and resources, contributing to carbon emissions and climate change.

On the other hand, reusable food containers are made from durable materials such as glass, stainless steel, or silicone, and can be used multiple times. They are often more robust and secure than disposable containers, protecting food from spills and leaks.

Reusable containers also come in various sizes and shapes, making them versatile and suitable for different types of food and occasions.

Using a reusable food container offers several benefits beyond environmental considerations. For example, they can save you money in the long run, as you won't need to purchase disposable containers regularly. Additionally, reusable containers are often safer for food storage than disposable ones, as they are typically free from harmful chemicals such as BPA or phthalates.

To make the switch to reusable food containers, consider investing in a few high-quality containers that suit your needs. Look for containers that are easy to clean, leak-proof, and of an appropriate size. You may also want to consider purchasing reusable utensils and straws to further reduce your reliance on single-use plastics.

When using reusable containers, be sure to clean them thoroughly after each use to prevent bacterial growth and contamination. Many reusable containers are dishwasher safe, making cleaning easy and convenient.

In conclusion, using a reusable food container instead of a disposable one is a simple but effective way to reduce waste and protect the environment.

Number 57: Cut down on medical expenses

Healthcare is a necessity in our lives, but it can also be expensive. Medical expenses can quickly add up, especially if you have a chronic illness or require frequent medical care. However, there are steps you can take to reduce your medical expenses and save money in the long run. One of the most effective ways to do this is by staying healthy and preventing illnesses.

Preventive care is essential in maintaining good health and reducing medical expenses. For instance, getting regular check-ups and screenings can help detect potential health problems early on and prevent them from worsening. This can save you from costly treatments and procedures down the road. Additionally, vaccinations can protect you from infectious diseases, which can be expensive to treat and may result in missed workdays.

Eating a healthy diet and exercising regularly can also help you stay healthy and prevent illnesses. A nutritious diet can help prevent chronic diseases, such as diabetes and heart disease, while exercise can strengthen your immune system and reduce your risk of developing certain health conditions. By maintaining a healthy lifestyle, you can reduce your medical expenses and also improve your quality of life.

Another way to prevent illnesses is by practicing good hygiene. Washing your hands regularly, avoiding close contact with sick individuals, and covering your mouth when you cough or sneeze can help prevent the spread of germs and viruses. This can reduce your risk of getting sick and also prevent the need for medical care.

Finally, it's important to manage any chronic health conditions you may have. This includes taking your medications as prescribed, monitoring your symptoms, and seeking medical care when necessary. By managing your health conditions, you can prevent complications and reduce your medical expenses over time.

In conclusion, staying healthy and preventing illnesses is a crucial step in reducing medical expenses. By practicing preventive care, eating a healthy diet, exercising regularly, practicing good hygiene, and managing chronic conditions, you can save money on medical care and improve your overall health and well-being. Remember, prevention is key, and taking care of your health now can save you money and stress in the long run.

Number 58: Use a reusable cloth towel instead of paper towels

Paper towels are widely used for cleaning purposes and are often considered a convenient option. However, they are also a major contributor to environmental pollution. The production of paper towels involves the cutting down of trees and the use of chemicals to bleach and process the paper, which pollutes the air and water. Additionally, paper towels are not easily biodegradable and often end up in landfills, taking years to decompose.

Using a reusable cloth towel, on the other hand, is a more sustainable option. Cloth towels can be used repeatedly, reducing the amount of waste generated. They are also easy to wash and maintain, and can be used for a variety of cleaning tasks.

Here are some of the benefits of using a reusable cloth towel:

1. Saves money - Over time, using a reusable cloth towel can save you money as you won't need to keep buying paper towels.

2. Reduces waste - By using a reusable cloth towel, you are reducing the amount of waste generated and helping the environment.

3. More absorbent - Cloth towels are typically more absorbent than paper towels, making them ideal for cleaning up spills or messes.

4. Eco-friendly - Cloth towels are made from natural materials and are biodegradable, making them a more eco-friendly option.

5. Versatile - Cloth towels can be used for a variety of cleaning tasks, including wiping counters, cleaning spills, and drying dishes.

In conclusion, using a reusable cloth towel instead of paper towels is a simple yet effective way to reduce your environmental impact. It saves money, reduces waste, and is a more eco-friendly option. So, next time you need to clean up a mess, reach for a cloth towel instead of a paper towel. Your efforts may seem small, but they can have a big impact on the environment.

Number 59: Use a reusable cloth coffee filter instead of disposables

Disposable coffee filters are a common choice for many coffee drinkers. But did you know that these filters are not only wasteful but also harmful to the environment? They contribute to the ever-growing problem of single-use plastic waste, which can take hundreds of years to decompose.

Thankfully, there's a simple solution to this problem – using a reusable cloth coffee filter. Not only is it a more eco-friendly option, but it also produces a better-tasting cup of coffee.

Here are some of the benefits of using a reusable cloth coffee filter:

1. It's environmentally friendly

By switching to a cloth filter, you can significantly reduce your carbon footprint. You won't have to throw away a filter after every use, which means less waste in landfills. Moreover, you won't have to worry about the environmental impact of producing and transporting disposable filters.

2. It's cost-effective

While a cloth coffee filter may seem like a more expensive option upfront, it is actually more cost-effective in the long run. You only need to buy a reusable filter once, and it can last for years with proper care. You won't have to keep buying disposable filters, which can add up over time.

3. It produces better-tasting coffee

Using a cloth filter can enhance the flavor of your coffee. Unlike paper filters, cloth filters allow more oils and flavors to seep into your cup, resulting in a fuller and richer taste. Additionally, the fabric filters out any sediments, producing a cleaner cup of coffee.

4. It's easy to clean

Cleaning a cloth coffee filter is a breeze. All you need to do is rinse it with water after each use and toss it in the washing machine once a week. It's that simple.

In conclusion, using a reusable cloth coffee filter is a small but impactful step towards a more sustainable future. It's a simple swap that can make a significant difference in the amount of waste we produce.

Number 60: Cut down on cleaning costs by making it yourself

Cleaning your home can be a costly affair, especially if you rely solely on store-bought cleaning products. However, you can significantly reduce your cleaning expenses by using homemade cleaning products. Not only are they affordable, but they are also effective and environmentally friendly.

Here are some homemade cleaning products that you can use to cut down on home cleaning expenses:

1. Vinegar and Baking Soda

Vinegar and baking soda are two of the most common ingredients in homemade cleaning products. They are affordable and readily available in most households. You can use vinegar and baking soda to clean your bathroom, kitchen, and other surfaces in your home.

To clean your toilet, pour one cup of vinegar into the bowl and let it sit for a few minutes. Then, sprinkle baking soda on the inside of the bowl and scrub with a toilet brush. Rinse with water, and your toilet will be sparkling clean.

To clean your kitchen sink, sprinkle baking soda on the surface, followed by vinegar. Scrub with a sponge or brush, and rinse with water. Your sink will be clean and fresh-smelling.

2. Lemon Juice

Lemon juice is a natural disinfectant and can be used to clean a variety of surfaces in your home. It is particularly effective in removing stains and grime from your kitchen countertops and cutting boards.

To clean your kitchen countertops, cut a lemon in half and rub it on the surface. Let the lemon juice sit for a few minutes, and then wipe with a damp cloth. Your countertops will be clean and free of germs.

3. Castile Soap

Castile soap is a natural soap made from vegetable oil and is a versatile cleaning product.

In conclusion, using homemade cleaning products is an effective way to cut down on your home cleaning expenses. Not only are they affordable, but they are also environmentally friendly and safe to use. Try out these homemade cleaning products today and enjoy a clean and fresh-smelling home.

Number 61: Use a reusable dusting cloth instead of disposables

Reusable dusting cloths are made of natural materials such as cotton and microfiber. These materials are environmentally friendly and can be washed and reused multiple times. Unlike disposable dusting cloths, reusable cloths do not require constant replacement, which reduces the amount of waste generated. Using reusable dusting cloths is a simple and cost-effective way to reduce the environmental impact of dusting.

The benefits of using reusable dusting cloths extend beyond environmental conservation. These cloths are more effective in cleaning than disposable ones. They are made of high-quality materials that can trap dust and other particles effectively. This means that fewer passes are required to clean the surface, which saves time and energy.

Additionally, reusable dusting cloths are more convenient to use than disposable ones. They are available in different sizes and shapes, which makes them suitable for cleaning different surfaces. They are also durable, which means they can withstand multiple washes without losing their effectiveness. This makes them a better investment in the long run than disposable dusting cloths.

Switching to reusable dusting cloths is a small change that can make a big difference in conserving the environment. By reducing the amount of waste generated, we can help to protect the planet for future generations. Furthermore, using reusable dusting cloths is a cost-effective and convenient way to clean our homes effectively.

In conclusion, using reusable dusting cloths is an effective way to reduce the environmental impact of dusting. It is a small change that can make a big difference in protecting the planet.
By choosing to use natural materials that are durable and effective, we can save money and time while conserving the environment.

Number 62: Cut down on lawn care expenses by doing it yourself

Maintaining a lush and green lawn can be a time-consuming and expensive task. Many homeowners opt to hire professional lawn care services to keep their yards looking their best. However, with a little effort and know-how, you can cut down on your lawn care expenses by doing it yourself.

Invest in Quality Equipment

The first step in maintaining your lawn is to invest in quality equipment. A decent lawn mower, trimmer, and edger are essential tools for keeping your lawn looking neat and tidy. While it may be tempting to go for the cheapest options, investing in quality equipment will save you both time and money in the long run. Cheap equipment is more likely to break down, leading to costly repairs or replacements.

Mow Regularly and Properly

Mowing is one of the essential tasks in lawn care. Regular mowing helps to keep your lawn healthy and looking neat. However, it's important to mow properly. Cutting your grass too short or too often can damage your lawn and lead to weed growth. Make sure to mow at the right height for your grass type and use a sharp blade to prevent tearing the grass.

Water Your Lawn Efficiently

Watering your lawn is essential for keeping it healthy, but it can also be costly. To save money on your water bill, it's important to water your lawn efficiently. This means watering deeply but infrequently, rather than frequently and shallowly. You can also invest in a timer or a rain sensor to ensure that your sprinkler system only runs when needed.

Control Weeds and Pests Naturally

Weeds and pests can quickly take over a lawn if left unchecked. Many homeowners opt to use chemical treatments to control these issues, but these can be harmful to the environment and your family's health. Instead, try using natural methods such as hand-weeding, using organic fertilizers, and introducing beneficial insects into your yard to control pests.

In conclusion, maintaining a beautiful lawn doesn't have to break the bank. By investing in quality equipment, learning the basics of lawn care, mowing regularly and properly, watering efficiently, and controlling weeds and pests naturally, you can save money while still enjoying a lush and green lawn. Plus, taking care of your lawn yourself can be a rewarding and satisfying experience.

Number 63: Use a reusable cloth mop instead of disposables

Using a reusable cloth mop is a simple and easy solution to the problem of disposable mop pads. A reusable cloth mop is made of durable and washable fabric that can be used over and over again. Unlike disposable mop pads, which are made of synthetic materials, reusable cloth mops are made of natural materials such as cotton or microfiber. This makes them eco-friendly and biodegradable.

The benefits of using a reusable cloth mop are numerous. Firstly, they are cost-effective. While disposable mop pads need to be replaced after every use, a reusable cloth mop can be used multiple times before needing to be washed. This means that over time, a reusable cloth mop can save you money and reduce your cleaning expenses.

Secondly, using a reusable cloth mop reduces waste. Disposable mop pads are made of non-biodegradable materials such as plastic and take hundreds of years to decompose. By using a reusable cloth mop, you are helping to reduce the amount of waste that goes into landfills.

Thirdly, reusable cloth mops are more effective at cleaning. They are made of high-quality materials that can easily absorb dirt and grime. Unlike disposable mop pads, which can leave streaks and residue on floors, reusable cloth mops leave floors looking clean and shiny.

Lastly, using a reusable cloth mop is a more sustainable choice. It reduces the use of natural resources, such as fossil fuels, which are used in the production and transportation of disposable mop pads. By using a reusable cloth mop, you are contributing to the preservation of natural resources and reducing your carbon footprint.

In conclusion, using a reusable cloth mop is a simple and effective way to save the environment. It is cost-effective, reduces waste, is more effective at cleaning, and is a sustainable choice. So, the next time you need to clean your floors, consider using a reusable cloth mop instead of disposable mop pads. It is a small step that can make a big difference.

Number 64: Cut down on car expenses by maintaining your vehicle

As a car owner, one of the most significant expenses you will face is the cost of maintaining your vehicle. However, regular car maintenance can help you save money in the long run by preventing major repairs and improving fuel efficiency. Here are some tips for cutting down on car expenses by regularly maintaining your vehicle.

1. Change the oil and air filter regularly
Oil is the lifeblood of your car's engine, and it is essential to change it regularly to keep your engine running smoothly. A dirty air filter can also reduce fuel efficiency and increase emissions, so it is important to replace it regularly.

2. Keep your tires properly inflated

Underinflated tires can decrease fuel efficiency and cause unnecessary wear and tear on your tires. Make sure to check your tire pressure regularly and inflate them to the recommended level.

3. Check your brakes regularly
Brakes are one of the most critical safety features on your car, and it is essential to keep them in good condition. Regularly checking your brake pads and rotors can prevent costly repairs and ensure that your car stops when you need it to.

4. Replace worn-out parts
If you notice any signs of wear and tear on your car, such as squeaking brakes or a vibrating steering wheel, it is essential to get it checked out by a mechanic. Replacing worn-out parts can prevent further damage and save you money on repairs in the long run.

5. Get regular tune-ups
Regular tune-ups can keep your car running smoothly and efficiently. A professional mechanic can detect any potential problems before they become major issues, saving you money on repairs.

By following these tips, you can cut down on car expenses by regularly maintaining your vehicle. Not only will this save you money in the long run, but it will also ensure that your car is safe and reliable on the road. Remember to always follow the manufacturer's recommended maintenance schedule and don't neglect any signs of wear and tear on your car.

Number 65: Use a reusable dish cloth instead of disposables

One small change that we can all make in our daily lives to reduce waste and save money is to switch from using disposable dish cloths to reusable ones. Disposable dish cloths may seem convenient, but they are actually harmful to the environment and can end up costing you more money in the long run. Here are some reasons why you should consider using reusable dish cloths instead of disposables.

Firstly, disposable dish cloths are made from materials such as paper or synthetic fibers that cannot be recycled. This means that every time you use a disposable dish cloth, you are contributing to the growing amount of waste in landfills. On the other hand, reusable dish cloths are usually made from natural materials such as cotton or linen, which can be washed and reused multiple times.

Secondly, using disposable dish cloths can end up costing you more money in the long run. While it may seem cheaper to buy a pack of disposable dish cloths, they don't last very long and you will need to buy them again and again. In contrast, reusable dish cloths can be washed and used over and over again, saving you money in the long run.

Finally, using reusable dish cloths is better for the environment. By using a reusable dish cloth, you are reducing the amount of waste that is sent to landfills and conserving natural resources that are used to make disposable products. Additionally, using a reusable dish cloth can help reduce your carbon footprint by cutting down on the transportation and production of disposable products.

In conclusion, using a reusable dish cloth instead of disposable ones is a small but important step that we can all take to reduce waste and save money.

Number 66: Cut down on water bills by taking shorter showers

As the world's population continues to grow, the demand for water is also increasing. Unfortunately, the amount of water available for use is limited. This has led to a surge in the cost of water, which has resulted in higher water bills for households. While there are many ways to reduce water usage, one of the easiest ways is by taking shorter showers.

The average shower lasts about eight minutes, and during this time, a lot of water is wasted. According to the Environmental Protection Agency (EPA), the average showerhead uses 2.5 gallons of water per minute. This means that an eight-minute shower uses around 20 gallons of water. If a person takes a five-minute shower instead, they can save 10 gallons of water per day, which is 3,650 gallons per year.

Apart from the environmental benefits of conserving water, taking shorter showers can also help reduce water bills. By using less water, households can save money on their monthly water bills. With the average water bill in the United States being around $70 per month, reducing shower time can lead to significant savings.

In addition to reducing water usage and saving money, taking shorter showers also has health benefits. Hot water can strip the skin of its natural oils, leading to dryness and irritation. By taking shorter showers, the skin is exposed to less hot water, which helps to retain moisture and prevent dryness.

To encourage shorter showers, households can install low-flow showerheads. These showerheads use less water per minute, without compromising on water pressure or quality. Some low-flow showerheads can reduce water usage by up to 50%, which can lead to significant water and cost savings.

In conclusion, taking shorter showers is an easy way to reduce water usage, save money, and promote better skin health. With the availability of low-flow showerheads, households can enjoy a comfortable shower experience while conserving water and reducing their bills.

Number 67: Use a reusable cloth sponge instead of disposables

A cloth sponge is typically made of cotton or microfiber and can be washed and reused multiple times. They are just as effective as traditional sponges, but they don't contribute to the plastic waste problem. A cloth sponge can be used for several months before needing to be replaced, depending on the frequency of use and how well it is cared for.

One of the biggest benefits of using a reusable cloth sponge is the cost savings. Traditional sponges are relatively inexpensive, but they need to be replaced frequently, which can add up over time. In contrast, a cloth sponge can be washed and reused, so it is a one-time investment that will save money in the long run.

Using a cloth sponge can also help reduce the amount of waste that ends up in landfills. According to the Environmental Protection Agency, sponges are not recyclable and can take hundreds of years to break down in a landfill. By using a reusable cloth sponge, you can help reduce your household waste and lessen your environmental impact.

Another benefit of using a cloth sponge is that it is easy to clean and maintain. Simply rinse it out after each use, and toss it in the washing machine when it starts to get dirty. A cloth sponge can also be sterilized by boiling it in hot water or microwaving it for a few seconds. This makes it a more hygienic option than traditional sponges that can harbor bacteria and germs.

In conclusion, using a reusable cloth sponge is an easy and effective way to reduce waste and save money. It is a small change that can make a big difference in the long run. By making this switch, you can help reduce the amount of plastic waste that ends up in landfills and contribute to a cleaner and healthier planet.

Number 68: Cut down on cell phone expenses by using prepaid plan

Cell phone bills can be expensive, and for many people, it can be challenging to keep up with the monthly payments. If you're looking to save some money on your phone bill, one option to consider is switching to a prepaid phone plan.

A prepaid phone plan is a type of phone service that requires you to pay upfront for the minutes, texts, and data you use. Unlike traditional phone plans, there are no contracts or monthly bills with prepaid plans. You can purchase a prepaid phone plan card or refill your account online, and the funds will be added to your account balance. As you use your phone, the cost of each call, text, or data usage is deducted from your balance.

One of the most significant advantages of a prepaid phone plan is that it can help you save money. With traditional phone plans, you may end up paying for services that you don't use, such as unlimited data or extra minutes. With a prepaid plan, you only pay for what you need, so you can avoid unnecessary costs.

Another benefit of using a prepaid phone plan is that there are no credit checks or contracts required. This makes it an ideal option for people who have poor credit or who don't want to commit to a long-term contract. It also means that you can switch between phone carriers easily if you find a better deal elsewhere.

If you're considering switching to a prepaid phone plan, there are a few things to keep in mind. First, you'll need to purchase an unlocked phone or one that is compatible with the prepaid plan you choose. Second, you'll need to monitor your usage carefully to avoid running out of minutes or data. Finally, some prepaid plans may have limitations, such as slower data speeds or fewer features than traditional phone plans.

In conclusion, if you're looking to cut down on your cell phone expenses, a prepaid phone plan may be a good option to consider. It can help you save money, avoid contracts and credit checks, and give you more control over your usage. Just be sure to choose a plan that meets your needs and monitor your usage carefully to avoid any unexpected charges.

Number 69: Use a reusable cloth duster instead of disposables

A reusable cloth duster is an eco-friendly alternative to disposable dusters. They are made of washable materials, such as cotton or microfiber, that can be used multiple times before needing to be washed. They are also durable and can withstand multiple washes, making them a cost-effective option in the long run.

Using a reusable cloth duster has a positive impact on the environment. By using a reusable duster, you reduce the amount of waste produced in your home. Instead of adding to the ever-growing landfills, you are reducing your carbon footprint by reusing your cleaning tools. Additionally, by using a reusable duster, you are not contributing to the demand for disposable cleaning tools, which means fewer resources are used in the production of these disposable items.

Using a reusable cloth duster also has health benefits. Disposable dusters can contain harsh chemicals that can be harmful to your health and the environment. By using a reusable duster, you eliminate the risk of exposing yourself and your family to these chemicals. You also reduce the number of chemicals released into the environment and help reduce pollution.

Switching to a reusable cloth duster is an easy step towards living a more sustainable lifestyle. It is a small change that has a big impact on the environment. It is also a cost-effective option that saves you money in the long run. By using a reusable duster, you are reducing your carbon footprint, protecting your health, and contributing to a cleaner, more sustainable future.

In conclusion, choosing a reusable cloth duster over a disposable one is a simple but effective way to reduce your environmental impact.

Number 70: Cut down Internet expenses by negotiating

In today's digital age, the internet has become an essential utility that most of us cannot live without. However, the cost of internet service can add up quickly and become a significant expense, especially if you are on a tight budget. Fortunately, there are ways to cut down your internet expenses, and one of them is by negotiating with your service provider.

Negotiating with your internet service provider can be intimidating, but it is worth the effort. Here are some tips to help you negotiate a better deal:

1. Research the competition

Before you start negotiating with your provider, do some research on their competitors in your area. Find out what deals and promotions they are offering to new customers. Armed with this knowledge, you can approach your provider with confidence and leverage the competition as a bargaining tool.

2. Know your current plan

Make sure you know your current plan and the services you are paying for. This will help you identify areas where you can negotiate a better deal. For example, if you are paying for a higher internet speed than you need, you can ask your provider to switch you to a cheaper plan.

3. Be prepared to negotiate

Your provider may offer you a discount or a promotional rate if you agree to extend your contract or bundle your services. Be prepared to negotiate and don't be afraid to ask for a better deal.

4. Be willing to switch providers

If your provider refuses to offer you a better deal, be prepared to switch to a competitor. Let your provider know that you are considering switching and see if they are willing to match or beat the competitor's offer.

Negotiating with your internet service provider can be a great way to save money on your monthly bills. By doing your research, knowing your current plan, and being prepared to negotiate, you can potentially lower your internet expenses and free up more money for other important expenses.

Number 71: Use a reusable face mask instead of disposables

The COVID-19 pandemic has brought about a new normal where wearing face masks is becoming a necessity to prevent the spread of the virus. As a result, disposable face masks have become a common sight in public spaces. However, the use of disposable face masks has raised environmental concerns due to their short lifespan and the amount of waste they generate. The good news is that there is an alternative – reusable face masks.

Reusable face masks are a more sustainable option as they can be used multiple times, reducing the amount of waste generated. They are also cost-effective in the long run as they eliminate the need to constantly purchase disposable masks. In addition, reusable face masks are often made from eco-friendly materials such as organic cotton or bamboo, making them even more environmentally friendly.

Another advantage of reusable face masks is that they can be washed and sanitized, ensuring that they remain hygienic for future use. This is particularly important for people who need to wear masks for extended periods of time, such as healthcare workers or those with compromised immune systems.

Using reusable face masks also supports local businesses as many small businesses have pivoted to produce reusable face masks in response to the pandemic. By purchasing from these businesses, we are supporting our local communities and reducing our carbon footprint by avoiding products that are shipped from overseas.

It is important to note that not all reusable face masks are created equal. It is essential to choose a mask that fits properly and provides adequate protection. The mask should cover both the nose and mouth and fit snugly against the face without being too tight. It is also important to choose a mask made from breathable materials to ensure comfort during extended use.

In conclusion, the use of reusable face masks is a simple yet effective way to reduce our impact on the environment. By choosing reusable face masks, we can reduce waste, support local businesses, and protect ourselves and others from the spread of COVID-19. It is a small change that can have a big impact on the health of our planet and our communities.

Number 72: Cut laundry expenses by washing in cold water

Laundry is an essential household chore, but it can also be an expensive one. Between the cost of detergent, fabric softener, and the energy required to run the washing machine, the cost of doing laundry can quickly add up. However, there is a simple solution to cutting down laundry expenses: washing clothes in cold water.

Many people believe that washing clothes in hot water is necessary to get them clean, but this is not the case. In fact, washing clothes in cold water can be just as effective, while also being gentler on your clothes and the environment.

One of the main reasons why washing clothes in hot water is more expensive is because it requires more energy. Heating water is one of the most energy-intensive processes that a washing machine can perform, and it can account for up to 90% of the energy used during a wash cycle. By washing clothes in cold water, you can significantly reduce the amount of energy required to do a load of laundry.

Another benefit of washing clothes in cold water is that it can help extend the life of your clothes. Hot water can be harsh on fabrics, causing them to fade, shrink, and wear out more quickly. Cold water, on the other hand, is gentler and less likely to cause damage to your clothes. This can save you money in the long run by reducing the need to replace clothes that have been damaged in the wash.

Washing clothes in cold water can also be better for the environment. By reducing the amount of energy required to do a load of laundry, you are also reducing your carbon footprint. This is especially important if you live in an area where electricity is generated from fossil fuels, as the production of electricity is a significant source of greenhouse gas emissions.

If you are looking to cut down on your laundry expenses, washing clothes in cold water is an easy and effective way to do so. Not only can it save you money on energy and detergent, but it can also help extend the life of your clothes and reduce your impact on the environment. So next time you do a load of laundry, consider turning down the temperature and see the savings for yourself.

Number 73: Use a reusable produce bag instead of plastic bags

Plastic bags have become a ubiquitous part of our daily lives. From grocery shopping to carrying our lunch to work, we use plastic bags for almost everything. However, the overuse of plastic bags is causing severe damage to our environment, and it's time to switch to a more sustainable and eco-friendly option - reusable produce bags.

Plastic bags are made of non-biodegradable materials that can take up to 1,000 years to decompose. They are not only harmful to the environment but also pose a significant threat to wildlife. Animals often mistake plastic bags for food and ingest them, leading to severe health issues and even death. Additionally, plastic bags are a significant contributor to ocean pollution, threatening marine life and habitats.

Reusable produce bags are a sustainable alternative to single-use plastic bags. They are made of durable materials like cotton or mesh and can be used multiple times. They come in various sizes and are ideal for carrying fruits and vegetables, bulk items, and even bread.

Using reusable produce bags can significantly reduce the number of plastic bags that end up in landfills and oceans. It's estimated that a single reusable produce bag can replace up to 1,000 plastic bags in its lifetime. By making a simple switch to reusable bags, we can drastically reduce our plastic waste and protect the environment.

Furthermore, reusable produce bags are easy to clean and maintain. They can be washed by hand or in a washing machine and are quick to dry. Unlike plastic bags, they don't tear or break, and they can be reused for years, making them a cost-effective option in the long run.

In conclusion, the overuse of plastic bags is causing severe damage to our planet, and we must reduce our waste.

Number 74: Cut down on gym expenses by working out at home

Going to the gym can be expensive, especially if you're on a tight budget. Luckily, there are plenty of ways to cut down on gym expenses by working out at home or outside.

One of the best ways to save money on gym expenses is by working out at home. With the rise of online fitness programs and YouTube workout videos, it's easier than ever to get a workout in from the comfort of your own home. Many online fitness programs offer free trial periods or low-cost monthly subscriptions, making it easy to find a program that fits your budget.

If you're not interested in online fitness programs, there are plenty of other ways to work out at home. You can purchase inexpensive workout equipment, such as resistance bands or dumbbells, or even use household items, like water bottles or cans, as weights. Bodyweight exercises, such as push-ups, squats, and lunges, can also provide a great workout without any equipment.

Another way to cut down on gym expenses is by working out outside. Going for a run or hike, biking, or doing yoga in the park are all great ways to get a workout in while enjoying the great outdoors. Many cities also offer free outdoor fitness classes, such as yoga or boot camps, which can be a fun and cost-effective way to switch up your workout routine.

Working out at home or outside not only saves you money on gym expenses, but it also offers many other benefits. You can work out on your own schedule, without having to worry about commuting to the gym. You also have the freedom to wear whatever you want and can avoid the crowds and distractions of a gym environment.

While working out at home or outside may not provide the same level of equipment or social atmosphere as a gym, it can still be an effective and enjoyable way to stay fit and save money. By finding a workout routine that works for you, you can achieve your fitness goals without breaking the bank.

Number 75: Use a reusable make up pad instead of disposables

the environment

Makeup remover pads are an essential part of any beauty routine. They help remove makeup, dirt, and oil from the face, leaving the skin clean and refreshed. However, the use of disposable makeup remover pads is a major contributor to environmental pollution. These pads are made from non-biodegradable materials like cotton and polyester, and they end up in landfills, where they take years to decompose. In addition, the production of disposable pads requires a lot of energy and resources, which further harms the environment. Fortunately, there is a solution to this problem: reusable makeup remover pads.

Reusable makeup remover pads are made from sustainable materials like organic cotton, bamboo, or hemp. They are designed to be washed and reused, which makes them an eco-friendly alternative to disposable pads. By using reusable pads, you can significantly reduce your environmental footprint and help preserve the planet for future generations.

Here are some of the benefits of using reusable makeup remover pads:

1. They are cost-effective

While reusable pads may seem more expensive than disposable pads at first, they are actually more cost-effective in the long run. You only need to buy them once, and you can reuse them for months or even years. This means you won't have to keep buying disposable pads, which can add up over time.

2. They are gentle on the skin

Reusable pads are soft and gentle on the skin, unlike some disposable pads that can be rough and abrasive. This means they are less likely to cause irritation or breakouts, making them ideal for people with sensitive skin.

3. They are easy to use and clean

Reusable pads are easy to use and clean. Simply wet the pad with water or your favorite makeup remover, and gently wipe your face to remove makeup. After use, rinse the pad with water and hand or machine wash it with your regular laundry. They are also quick-drying, which means you can reuse them again in no time.

In conclusion, using reusable makeup remover pads is a simple but effective way to reduce your environmental impact and promote sustainability.

Number 76: Cut down on car insurance expenses

1. Compare rates from different providers

The first step to finding affordable car insurance is to compare rates from different providers. You can do this online or by contacting insurance providers directly. It's essential to compare the same coverage options to get an accurate comparison of rates. You can also use online comparison tools that will do the work for you.

2. Look for discounts

Many insurance providers offer discounts to their customers. These can include safe driver discounts, multi-car discounts, and discounts for having multiple policies with the same provider. You should also look for discounts related to your driving habits, such as discounts for low mileage or for taking a defensive driving course.

3. Increase your deductible

Your deductible is the amount you pay out of pocket before your insurance kicks in. Increasing your deductible can lower your monthly premium. However, it's essential to make sure you have enough money set aside to cover the deductible in case of an accident.

4. Consider dropping coverage you don't need

If you have an older car, you may not need collision or comprehensive coverage, which can be costly. Consider dropping these coverages to reduce your premium.

5. Improve your credit score

Your credit score can affect your insurance premium. If you have a low credit score, you may be paying more for car insurance than someone with a higher score. Improving your credit score can help lower your premium.

In conclusion, cutting down on car insurance expenses is possible by shopping for better rates. Compare rates from different providers, look for discounts, increase your deductible, drop coverage you don't need, improve your credit score, avoid lapses in coverage, and drive safely. By following these tips, you can save money on car insurance without sacrificing coverage.

Number 77: Use a reusable shower cap instead of disposables

Disposable shower caps are a popular product in the market, and they are often used in hotels, spas, and homes. They are designed to be used once and then thrown away. While they may seem convenient, they are actually harmful to the environment. Disposable shower caps are made of plastic, and as we all know, plastic is a major contributor to pollution. When these shower caps are thrown away, they take hundreds of years to decompose, and during this time, they release harmful toxins into the environment.

On the other hand, reusable shower caps are an eco-friendly alternative that can help to reduce our carbon footprint. These shower caps are made of durable materials such as silicone or fabric, and they can be washed and reused multiple times. This means that they are a more sustainable option that can help to reduce the amount of waste that is produced.

In addition to being environmentally friendly, reusable shower caps also have other benefits. For example, they are often more comfortable to wear than disposable shower caps, as they are designed to fit snugly on the head without being too tight. They also come in a variety of colors and designs, which means that you can choose one that matches your personal style.

Another great thing about reusable shower caps is that they are affordable and cost-effective in the long run. While they may cost more upfront than disposable shower caps, they are a one-time investment that will last for years. This means that you won't have to keep buying new shower caps every time you need to use one.

In conclusion, using a reusable shower cap instead of a disposable one is a small change that can have a big impact on the environment. By making this switch, you can help to reduce the amount of plastic waste that is produced and contribute to a more sustainable future. So, next time you need a shower cap, consider investing in a reusable one – your wallet and the planet will thank you for it!

Number 78: Cut down on office expenses by using digital documents

The world is becoming more digitized each day, and businesses are not left out. One of the most significant ways companies can cut down on office expenses is by using digital documents instead of printing.

Printing documents can be quite expensive, and it's not just the cost of paper and ink that businesses have to worry about. There are also expenses like printer maintenance, electricity bills, and document storage. All these expenses can add up and become a significant burden on a company's finances.

However, when companies switch to digital documents, they can save thousands of dollars each year. Here are some ways digital documents can help businesses cut down on office expenses:

1. No need for printing equipment

When businesses switch to digital documents, they no longer need to invest in printing equipment like printers, copiers, and scanners. This means that businesses can save money on upfront costs and ongoing maintenance expenses.

2. Reduced paper usage

Printing documents requires paper, and paper costs can add up quickly. When businesses use digital documents, they no longer need to use paper. This can lead to significant savings over time.

3. Lower ink and toner expenses

Ink and toner can be costly, and businesses that print a lot of documents can quickly rack up expenses. When businesses switch to digital documents, they no longer need to purchase ink and toner, leading to significant cost savings.

In conclusion, switching to digital documents is an excellent way for businesses to cut down on office expenses. It can help businesses save money on printing equipment, paper, ink and toner, document storage, and energy bills. It's a win-win situation as businesses save money, and the environment benefits from reduced paper usage.

Number 79: Use a reusable sandwich bag instead of disposables

In today's world, we all need to be conscious of our impact on the environment. One easy way to reduce our environmental footprint is by using reusable sandwich bags instead of disposable ones. By doing so, we can save money, reduce waste, and help protect the planet.

Disposable sandwich bags are used once and then thrown away, adding to the growing problem of plastic pollution. According to the Environmental Protection Agency (EPA), Americans alone generate more than 4 million tons of plastic bags, wraps, and sacks annually, most of which ends up in landfills or oceans. These bags take hundreds of years to decompose, and as they do, they release harmful chemicals and microplastics into the environment.

Reusable sandwich bags, on the other hand, can be used over and over again. They are made of durable, washable materials such as silicone, cloth, or food-grade plastic. They come in a variety of sizes and designs, making them perfect for packing sandwiches, snacks, fruits, and vegetables. By using a reusable sandwich bag instead of a disposable one, you can save money in the long run, as you won't have to keep buying new bags.

Furthermore, reusable sandwich bags are more sustainable and eco-friendly. They reduce waste and conserve resources by eliminating the need for single-use plastics. They also help to reduce carbon emissions, as they are often made of materials that have a lower carbon footprint than disposable bags.

In addition to being environmentally friendly, reusable sandwich bags are also more convenient and practical. They are designed to be leak-proof, airtight, and easy to clean. They can be washed in the dishwasher or by hand, and they dry quickly. Some reusable sandwich bags are even freezer-safe, allowing you to pack meals in advance and store them for later.

Using a reusable sandwich bag is a small but impactful step towards a more sustainable lifestyle. It's a simple change that can make a big difference. So, the next time you pack your lunch, consider using a reusable sandwich bag instead of a disposable one.

Number 80: Cut down credit card interest by paying off debts ASAP

Credit cards are a convenient way to make purchases, but they also come with high-interest rates that can quickly add up. If you're carrying a balance on your credit card, you're likely paying a significant amount in interest charges each month. However, there is a way to cut down on credit card interest and save money in the long run – paying off your debts as soon as possible.

The first step to cutting down on credit card interest is to stop using your credit card. If you continue to use your credit card while carrying a balance, you'll add even more to your debt and increase your interest charges. Instead, focus on paying off your debts as soon as possible.

One effective way to pay off your credit card debt is to use the snowball method. This involves paying off the debt with the smallest balance first while making the minimum payments on your other debts. Once the smallest debt is paid off, move on to the next smallest debt and continue this process until all your debts are paid off. This method helps you gain momentum and motivation as you see progress in paying off your debts.

Another way to pay off your credit card debt is to transfer your balance to a card with a lower interest rate or a 0% introductory rate. This can help you save money on interest charges and allow you to pay off your debt faster. However, be aware of balance transfer fees and make sure to pay off the balance before the introductory period ends to avoid high-interest charges.

It's important to make every effort to pay more than the minimum payment on your credit card. The minimum payment only covers the interest charges and a small portion of the principal balance, which means it will take you much longer to pay off your debts. By paying more than the minimum payment, you'll pay off your debts faster and save money on interest charges.

In conclusion, cutting down credit card interest by paying off debts as soon as possible is a smart financial move. By stopping the use of your credit card, using the snowball method, transferring balances to a lower interest rate, and paying more than the minimum payment, you can save money and become debt-free sooner. Remember, it's crucial to stay disciplined and committed to paying off your debts to achieve financial freedom.

Number 81: Use a reusable snack bag instead of disposables

Reusable snack bags are made from durable materials such as silicone, cloth, or food-grade plastics that are easy to clean and maintain. They come in various sizes and designs to suit different preferences. They are an excellent alternative to single-use plastic bags because they not only reduce waste but also save money in the long run.

Using a reusable snack bag is an easy way to make a positive impact on the environment. By choosing to use a reusable snack bag instead of disposable bags, you can reduce the amount of plastic waste that ends up in landfills and oceans. This, in turn, reduces greenhouse gas emissions and helps to conserve natural resources.

Reusable snack bags are also a healthier option for you and your family. Unlike disposable bags, reusable bags do not contain harmful chemicals such as BPA, phthalates, or lead, which can leach into your food and cause health problems. They are also easy to clean and can be used multiple times, making them a more hygienic option.

Switching to reusable snack bags is a small step, but it can make a significant impact on the environment. It is an easy way to reduce your carbon footprint and help to protect the planet. There are many reusable snack bags available online and in stores, so it is easy to find one that suits your needs and preferences.

In conclusion, using a reusable snack bag instead of disposable bags is a simple and effective way to reduce waste and protect the environment. It is a small change that can make a big difference. By choosing to use a reusable snack bag, you are taking a step towards a more sustainable and eco-friendly lifestyle.

Number 82: Cut down home insurance expenses with better rates

As a homeowner, one of the essential expenses you will need to budget for is your home insurance. This insurance policy protects you from financial loss in the event of damage or loss of your property, including your home and personal belongings. However, the cost of home insurance can be quite high, especially if you have a high-value property or live in an area prone to natural disasters. But did you know that you can cut down on your home insurance expenses by looking for better rates? Here is how to go about it.

Shop Around for Better Rates

One of the most effective ways to reduce your home insurance expenses is to shop around for better rates. This involves comparing quotes from different insurance companies to find the best deal. You can start by contacting your current insurance company to see if they can offer you a better rate. If not, you can look for other insurers who offer better rates. You can also use online comparison tools to compare quotes from different insurance companies.

Bundle Policies

Another way to reduce your home insurance expenses is to bundle policies. This involves combining your home insurance policy with other insurance policies such as auto insurance or life insurance. Bundling policies can result in significant savings as insurance companies offer discounts for multiple policies.

Increase Your Deductibles

Your deductible is the amount you pay out of pocket before your insurance policy kicks in. Increasing your deductibles can help reduce your home insurance expenses. However, you need to ensure that you can afford to pay the deductible in case of an emergency.

Conclusion

Reducing your home insurance expenses is possible by shopping around for better rates, bundling policies, increasing your deductibles, improving your home security, and maintaining good credit. By implementing these strategies, you can save money on your home insurance without compromising on the coverage you need to protect your home and personal belongings.

Number 83: Use a reusable handkerchief instead of disposables

Handkerchiefs have been in use for centuries as a means of wiping away tears, sweat, and mucus. However, with the advent of disposable tissues and napkins, the use of handkerchiefs has declined. But with growing concerns about the environment and the need to reduce waste, using a reusable handkerchief is a smart and sustainable choice.

First and foremost, using a reusable handkerchief is a cost-effective option. A pack of disposable tissues may seem cheap, but they are designed to be used once and thrown away, which means that you have to keep buying them regularly. On the other hand, a single handkerchief can last for years, making it a one-time investment that saves money in the long run.

Moreover, reusable handkerchiefs are eco-friendly. According to research, about 8,000 metric tons of used tissues are discarded every day worldwide, which adds to the already overflowing landfills. These tissues take years to decompose, releasing harmful gases in the process. In contrast, handkerchiefs can be washed and reused multiple times, reducing the amount of waste generated.

Using a handkerchief is also a healthier option. Disposable tissues are often treated with chemicals that can irritate the skin and cause allergic reactions. Additionally, some tissues contain fragrances that can trigger respiratory problems in people with sensitive airways. A handkerchief, on the other hand, is made of soft cotton or silk, which is gentle on the skin and does not contain any harmful chemicals.

Finally, using a handkerchief is a stylish choice. There are many designs and patterns available in the market, ranging from floral prints to geometric shapes. You can choose one that matches your personality and style, making it a unique and personal accessory.

In conclusion, using a reusable handkerchief is a smart and sustainable choice that saves money and reduces waste. It is a healthier and stylish option that is gentle on the skin and the environment. So, next time you reach for a disposable tissue, consider using a handkerchief instead and make a small but significant contribution to the planet.

Number 84: Cut down health insurance expenses

Health insurance is a vital expense for many people, but the cost of premiums and deductibles can be a significant burden for some. One way to reduce these expenses is by staying healthy and preventing illnesses.

Staying healthy starts with a balanced diet, regular exercise, and adequate sleep. Eating a diet rich in fruits, vegetables, lean proteins, and whole grains can help reduce the risk of chronic diseases such as diabetes, heart disease, and cancer. Exercise can help maintain a healthy weight, strengthen muscles, and improve cardiovascular health. Finally, getting enough sleep is essential for physical and mental well-being.

Preventing illnesses also plays a critical role in reducing health insurance expenses. This includes getting regular check-ups and screenings for conditions such as high blood pressure, high cholesterol, and cancer. Vaccinations are also an essential preventative measure, as they can protect against diseases such as the flu, pneumonia, and shingles.

It is also important to avoid risky behaviors such as smoking and excessive alcohol consumption. Smoking is a leading cause of preventable death and can increase the risk of lung cancer, heart disease, and stroke. Excessive alcohol consumption can lead to liver disease, high blood pressure, and other health problems.

In addition to these measures, it is important to take advantage of any wellness programs offered by your health insurance provider.

Many insurers offer discounts or incentives for participating in programs such as weight management, smoking cessation, and stress reduction.

Finally, it is important to shop around for the best health insurance plan for your needs. Compare premiums, deductibles, and coverage options to find a plan that fits your budget and provides the coverage you need.

In conclusion, staying healthy and preventing illnesses can help reduce health insurance expenses. By eating a balanced diet, exercising regularly, getting enough sleep, and avoiding risky behaviors, you can maintain good health and reduce the risk of chronic diseases. Taking advantage of wellness programs offered by your insurer and shopping around for the best plan can also help reduce costs. By taking these steps, you can protect your health and your wallet.

Number 85: Use a reusable bib instead of disposables

As parents, we all want to provide the best for our children. However, as much as we want to give them everything, there are times when we need to be practical. One of the things that we can do to save money is to use a reusable bib instead of a disposable one.

Disposable bibs may seem convenient, but they can be quite costly in the long run. You may think that using a reusable bib is too much of an effort, but it's actually not. In fact, using a reusable bib is not only practical, but it's also eco-friendly.

Here are some reasons why you should consider using a reusable bib:

1. It's cost-effective

Disposable bibs may seem cheap when you buy them, but they can add up over time. If you calculate the cost of buying a pack of disposable bibs every week or every month, you'll realize that it's more expensive than buying a reusable bib. A reusable bib may cost more upfront, but it can last for a long time, which means you won't have to keep buying new bibs.

2. It's eco-friendly

Disposable bibs are made of plastic, which is not biodegradable. This means that they will take years to decompose and will contribute to environmental pollution. On the other hand, a reusable bib is made of fabric, which can be washed and reused multiple times. This reduces the amount of waste that goes into landfills.

3. It's easy to clean

Cleaning a reusable bib is not as difficult as it may seem. You can simply toss it in the washing machine with your regular laundry. You don't need to spend extra money on special detergents or cleaning products. This makes it a hassle-free option for busy parents.

In conclusion, using a reusable bib instead of a disposable one is a practical and eco-friendly choice. It may require a little more effort, but it's worth it in the long run. You'll save money, reduce waste, and provide your child with a more comfortable mealtime experience.

Number 86: Cut car maintenance costs by learning basic repairs

As a car owner, it's inevitable that you'll have to spend money on maintenance and repairs. However, learning basic car repairs can help you save money in the long run. Here are some tips on how to cut down car maintenance expenses by learning basic repairs.

1. Change Your Oil and Oil Filter: Oil changes are a crucial aspect of car maintenance that shouldn't be ignored. You can save a significant amount of money by doing it yourself. All you need is a few tools, the right oil, and an oil filter. Follow the manufacturer's instructions and be sure to dispose of the old oil properly.

2. Replace Your Air Filter: A dirty air filter can reduce your car's fuel efficiency and cause engine problems. Fortunately, changing your air filter is a straightforward process that only requires a few minutes of your time. You can save money by buying the filter yourself and installing it.

3. Replace Your Spark Plugs: Spark plugs are essential for the proper functioning of your engine. Over time, they wear out and need to be replaced. You can save money by buying the spark plugs yourself and replacing them at home. Just make sure you use the correct type of spark plug for your car.

4. Change Your Brake Pads: Worn brake pads can be dangerous and costly to replace. However, changing them yourself is a simple process that can save you a lot of money. You'll need a few tools and the right brake pads. Follow the manufacturer's instructions and take your time to ensure that you do it correctly.

5. Replace Your Battery: A dead battery can leave you stranded and can be costly to replace at a mechanic. However, replacing a battery is a simple process that you can do yourself. You'll need the right tools and a new battery. Follow the manufacturer's instructions and take your time to ensure that you do it correctly.

In conclusion, learning basic car repairs can help you save money on maintenance expenses. While some repairs may require more advanced knowledge, these simple repairs can be done by almost anyone with a little bit of patience and the right tools. By doing these repairs yourself, you can save money and have the satisfaction of knowing that you're taking care of your car.

Number 87: Use a reusable seat cover instead of disposables

Using a reusable seat cover instead of disposable ones to save money is a cost-effective and eco-friendly solution. Disposable seat covers are commonly used in many industries, such as automotive, aviation, and hospitality, to protect seats from dirt, spills, and stains. However, these disposable covers can add up to a significant expense over time and can also have a negative impact on the environment. By switching to reusable seat covers, you can save money and reduce your carbon footprint.

One of the main advantages of using reusable seat covers is their durability. Unlike disposable covers, which are made of thin, lightweight materials, reusable covers are designed to withstand multiple uses and washes. This means that you can use them repeatedly, without having to constantly replace them. This can save you a significant amount of money in the long run, especially if you frequently use seat covers.

Another benefit of reusable seat covers is their environmental impact. Disposable seat covers are often made of non-biodegradable materials, such as plastic or paper, which can take years to decompose. This means that they contribute to the growing problem of waste and pollution. By using reusable covers, you can reduce your reliance on disposable products and help to minimize your environmental impact.

Reusable seat covers are also easy to clean and maintain. Most reusable covers are machine washable, which means that you can simply toss them in the washing machine after each use. This makes them a convenient and hassle-free solution, compared to disposable covers, which often have to be disposed of after each use.

In addition to saving money and reducing waste, using reusable seat covers can also contribute to a more professional and polished appearance. Reusable covers are often made of high-quality materials and can be customized with your company's logo or branding. This can help to create a more cohesive and professional look, which can be beneficial for businesses in the hospitality or automotive industries.

Overall, using a reusable seat cover instead of disposable ones to save money is a smart and eco-friendly choice. By investing in high-quality, durable covers, you can reduce your expenses over time and minimize your impact on the environment. Whether you are a business owner or an individual, making the switch to reusable seat covers is a simple and effective way to save money and reduce waste.

Number 88: Cut down home security expenses with DIY

Home security is one of the most important things that homeowners should prioritize. However, traditional home security systems can be quite expensive. The good news is that there are ways to cut down home security expenses with DIY security measures.

Here are some DIY security measures that can help you save money:

1. Install a security camera

Installing a security camera is one of the most effective ways to secure your home. With a security camera, you can monitor your home 24/7 and deter potential burglars. The good news is that there are now affordable security cameras that you can install yourself. You can purchase a wireless security camera that you can connect to your home Wi-Fi network and access through a mobile app.

2. Install smart locks

Smart locks are another DIY security measure that can help you save money. These locks can be controlled through a mobile app, giving you the ability to lock and unlock your doors remotely. Smart locks are also more secure than traditional locks, as they use encryption technology to prevent hacking.

3. Use motion sensor lights

Motion sensor lights are an affordable way to deter potential burglars. These lights turn on automatically when they sense movement, which can startle intruders and make them think twice about breaking into your home. You can purchase motion sensor lights at your local hardware store and install them yourself.

4. Install window and door sensors

Window and door sensors are another affordable DIY security measure that can help you secure your home. These sensors detect when a window or door is opened and send an alert to your mobile device. You can purchase window and door sensors online or at your local hardware store.

In conclusion, there are many DIY security measures that can help you cut down on home security expenses. By installing a security camera, smart locks, motion sensor lights, window and door sensors, and using a fake security system sign, you can secure your home without breaking the bank.

Number 89: Use reusable swim diaper instead of disposables

Swimming is one of the most enjoyable activities for children and adults alike, especially during the hot summer months. It's a great way to cool off and have some fun in the sun. However, when it comes to swimming, diapers are a must for children who are not yet potty trained. As a result, many parents opt for disposable swim diapers, but there is another option that can save you money in the long run: reusable swim diapers.

Reusable swim diapers are washable, adjustable, and come in a variety of sizes and designs. They are made from materials such as polyester, nylon, or cotton, which means they can be washed and reused multiple times. Unlike disposable swim diapers, which are only used once and then thrown away, reusable swim diapers can be used again and again, making them a more sustainable and cost-effective option.

The cost of disposable swim diapers can add up quickly, especially if you're swimming frequently. On average, a pack of disposable swim diapers costs around $10-$15, and each pack contains around 10-12 diapers. If you swim once a week during the summer months, you could easily spend $100-$150 on disposable swim diapers alone. In contrast, a reusable swim diaper costs around $10-$20 and can be used for multiple swim sessions. This means that you could save hundreds of dollars by switching to a reusable swim diaper.

In addition to being cost-effective, reusable swim diapers are also environmentally friendly. Disposable swim diapers are not biodegradable and can take hundreds of years to decompose in landfills. This means that every disposable swim diaper that you use contributes to environmental pollution. In contrast, reusable swim diapers are washable and can be used for years, reducing the amount of waste that ends up in landfills.

Another advantage of using reusable swim diapers is that they are adjustable. Unlike disposable swim diapers, which come in specific sizes, reusable swim diapers have adjustable waistbands and leg openings. This means that you can adjust the diaper to fit your child perfectly, ensuring that there are no leaks or accidents while swimming.

In conclusion, using a reusable swim diaper instead of disposable ones can save you money in the long run. They are cost-effective, environmentally friendly, and adjustable, making them a great option for parents who want to reduce their environmental footprint and save money at the same time. So why not make the switch to reusable swim diapers and enjoy a more sustainable and affordable summer swim season?

Number 90: Cut down travel expenses by programs & rewards

As the world becomes more connected, travel has become an essential part of our lives. Whether it's for work or leisure, we need to travel from one place to another. However, frequent travel can be expensive, and the expenses can add up quickly. Fortunately, there are several ways to cut down travel expenses by using programs and rewards.

1. Loyalty Programs

One of the most effective ways to cut down travel expenses is by joining loyalty programs. Almost every airline, hotel, and car rental company has a loyalty program that offers rewards to frequent customers. These rewards can include free flights, hotel stays, car rentals, and upgrades.

To get the most out of loyalty programs, it's important to stick to one or two airlines, hotels, and car rental companies. By doing so, you can accumulate points and earn rewards faster. You can also earn more rewards by using a credit card that's affiliated with the loyalty program.

2. Credit Card Rewards

Credit card rewards can also help you cut down travel expenses. Many credit cards offer rewards points or cashback for every purchase you make. You can use these rewards to pay for travel expenses like flights, hotels, and car rentals.

To maximize credit card rewards, choose a card that offers rewards for travel-related purchases. Some cards also offer bonus rewards for signing up and spending a certain amount within the first few months.

3. Travel Booking Websites

Travel booking websites like Expedia, Travelocity, and Kayak can also help you save money on travel expenses. These websites offer discounts on flights, hotels, and car rentals. You can compare prices from different airlines, hotels, and car rental companies to find the best deal.

Some travel booking websites also offer rewards programs that allow you to earn points for every booking you make. These points can be redeemed for free flights, hotel stays, and rental cars.

In conclusion, cutting down travel expenses is possible by using programs and rewards. By joining loyalty programs, using credit card rewards, booking through travel booking websites, and purchasing travel insurance, you can save money on your next trip. With a little bit of planning and research, you can make your next trip more affordable and enjoyable.

Number 91: Use a reusable menstrual pad instead of disposables

Disposable menstrual pads are a major contributor to the waste in landfills. According to a report by the Women's Environmental Network, a woman will use around 11,000 disposable menstrual products in her lifetime. These products take years to decompose and release harmful chemicals into the environment. By using a reusable menstrual pad, you can significantly reduce the amount of waste you produce.

In addition to being better for the environment, reusable menstrual pads can also save you money. While the initial cost of a reusable pad may be higher than a disposable one, it is a one-time investment that can last for years. On average, a pack of disposable pads costs around $5-10, while a reusable pad can cost between $15-25. However, a reusable pad can last for up to 5 years with proper care, which means you will save hundreds of dollars in the long run.

Reusable pads are also more comfortable and healthier for your body. Disposable pads contain chemicals and synthetic materials that can cause irritation and even infections. Reusable pads are made from natural materials such as cotton, bamboo, and hemp, which are gentle on the skin and reduce the risk of irritation and infection.

Using a reusable menstrual pad is easy. Simply wash the pad with soap and water after each use, and then toss it in the washing machine with your regular laundry. It's important to follow the care instructions provided by the manufacturer to ensure the longevity of the pad.

In conclusion, switching to a reusable menstrual pad is a great way to reduce waste, save money, and take care of your body. It may take some getting used to, but the benefits are worth it. With reusable pads becoming more widely available, it's easier than ever to make the switch and do your part for the environment.

Number 92: Cut down home improvement costs by DIY projects

Home improvement projects can be expensive, but there are ways to cut down costs by doing DIY projects. DIY projects allow you to save money on labor costs and learn new skills in the process. Here are some tips on how to cut down home improvement costs by doing DIY projects.

1. Plan ahead

Before starting any DIY project, it's important to plan ahead. Make a list of materials and tools you'll need and compare prices at different stores. This will help you budget for the project and avoid overspending.

2. Do your research

Research is key when it comes to DIY projects. Take the time to read articles, watch videos, and ask for advice from friends or family members who have done similar projects. This will help you avoid mistakes and ensure that the project is done correctly.

3. Use recycled materials

Using recycled materials is a great way to save money on DIY projects. Look for items that can be repurposed, such as old furniture, pallets, or even scrap wood. Not only will this save you money, but it's also environmentally friendly.

4. Start with small projects

If you're new to DIY projects, start with small projects that are easy to complete. This will help you build your skills and confidence, and you'll be more likely to tackle bigger projects in the future.

5. Take advantage of free resources

There are many free resources available for DIY projects, such as online tutorials, community workshops, and home improvement classes. Take advantage of these resources to learn new skills and get inspiration for your projects.

In conclusion, there are many ways to cut down home improvement costs by doing DIY projects. With a little planning, research, and creativity, you can save money and create a home that reflects your personal style and taste.

Number 93: Use a reusable diaper cover instead of disposables

As a new parent, one of the biggest expenses is buying diapers for your little one. Disposable diapers can be expensive and can add up quickly, especially if you're changing your baby's diaper frequently. But there is an alternative that can save you money in the long run – reusable diaper covers.

Reusable diaper covers are a great way to save money and reduce waste. They are made from washable materials and can be used over and over again. Unlike disposable diapers, which need to be thrown away after each use, reusable diaper covers can be washed and reused multiple times.

Here are some of the benefits of using reusable diaper covers:

1. Cost-effective

One of the biggest advantages of using reusable diaper covers is the cost savings. While the initial investment in reusable diaper covers may be more expensive than buying disposable diapers, in the long run, you'll save money. You won't have to keep buying diapers every week, and you'll be able to reuse the diaper covers for months, if not years.

2. Environmentally friendly

Disposable diapers are a huge source of waste. It is estimated that it takes up to 500 years for a disposable diaper to decompose. By using reusable diaper covers, you'll be reducing the amount of waste that goes into landfills. Additionally, many reusable diaper covers are made from eco-friendly materials, such as organic cotton, bamboo, or hemp.

3. More comfortable for your baby

Reusable diaper covers are more breathable than disposable ones, which can help prevent diaper rash. They are also less likely to leak, which means your baby will stay dry and comfortable for longer periods.

In conclusion, if you're looking for a cost-effective and eco-friendly way to diaper your baby, reusable diaper covers are a great option. They are comfortable for your baby, easy to use, and come in a variety of fun patterns and colors. By making the switch to reusable diaper covers, you'll be saving money and reducing waste, all while keeping your baby happy and comfortable.

Number 94: Cut down car rental expenses by getting better rates

Travelling is an exciting experience, but it can also be expensive. One of the biggest expenses that travelers incur is car rental. However, there are ways to cut down on rental expenses by looking for better rates. In this article, we will discuss some tips on how to cut down on car rental expenses.

1. Shop around

The first step to cutting down on car rental expenses is to shop around for the best rates. There are several car rental companies out there, and each of them has different rates. By shopping around, you can compare the rates of different companies and choose the one that offers the best deal.

2. Use online travel agencies

Another way to cut down on car rental expenses is to use online travel agencies. These agencies have partnerships with car rental companies and can offer discounted rates. Some popular online travel agencies include Expedia, Orbitz, and Priceline.

3. Book in advance

Booking your car rental in advance can also help you save money. Car rental companies offer discounts for early bookings, so it's a good idea to book your rental car as soon as you know your travel dates.

4. Look for coupons and discounts

Many car rental companies offer coupons and discounts that can help you save money. Before booking your rental car, check the company's website for any available coupons or discounts. You can also search for coupons and discounts on third-party websites like RetailMeNot.

In conclusion, cutting down on car rental expenses is possible by looking for better rates. Shop around, use online travel agencies, book in advance, look for coupons and discounts, rent from a non-airport location, and choose the right car to save money on rental expenses.

Number 95: Use a reusable nursing pad instead of disposables

Reusable nursing pads are eco-friendly

Disposable nursing pads contribute to the growing problem of waste in landfills. They are used for a short period and then thrown away, which means they accumulate in landfills, taking years to decompose. On the other hand, reusable nursing pads can be used for an extended period. They can be washed and reused multiple times, reducing the amount of waste generated.

Reusable nursing pads are cost-effective

Disposable nursing pads can be quite expensive, especially if you need to use them for an extended period. The cost of buying a pack of disposable nursing pads can add up over time, and you may end up spending a significant amount of money. However, reusable nursing pads are cost-effective in the long run. While the initial cost of buying reusable nursing pads may be higher than buying disposable ones, you will save money in the long run because you can use them repeatedly.

Reusable nursing pads are comfortable

Reusable nursing pads are made of soft, absorbent material that is gentle on your skin. They are designed to fit comfortably on your breast, preventing any discomfort or irritation. Unlike disposable nursing pads, which can be bulky and uncomfortable, reusable nursing pads are thin and discreet, making them comfortable to wear.

Reusable nursing pads are easy to use

Using reusable nursing pads is easy and straightforward. You can wash them along with your regular laundry, and they dry quickly. You can also carry them with you in your diaper bag, so you always have a fresh pair on hand.

In conclusion, switching to reusable nursing pads is an excellent way to save money while also reducing your environmental impact. They are eco-friendly, cost-effective, comfortable, and easy to use. If you're a new mother looking for ways to save money, consider switching to reusable nursing pads. You'll not only save money and reduce your environmental impact, but you'll also enjoy the comfort and convenience they provide.

Number 96: Cut down salon expenses by DIY

Beauty salons are a great place to get pampered and look your best, but the costs of regular treatments can add up quickly. From haircuts and coloring to manicures and pedicures, the prices can be steep. However, by learning some DIY hair and nail care techniques, you can save a significant amount of money while still looking great.

DIY Hair Care

One of the easiest ways to save money on hair care is to learn how to cut your own hair. While it may seem daunting at first, with a bit of practice and the right tools, it can be a great way to save money and keep your hair looking great. There are many tutorials and guides available online that can help you get started.

Another way to save money on hair care is to skip the expensive salon treatments and opt for DIY alternatives. For example, instead of getting a keratin treatment, you can use a DIY hair mask made from ingredients like coconut oil and honey. These natural treatments can help to condition and strengthen your hair without the hefty price tag.

DIY Nail Care

Manicures and pedicures can be another expensive beauty salon expense. However, with a bit of practice, you can learn to do your own nails at home. Start by investing in some basic nail care tools, such as a nail file, cuticle remover, and nail polish. There are also many DIY nail art tutorials available online that can help you create beautiful designs at home.

Another way to save money on nail care is to invest in quality nail products that can be used at home. For example, instead of getting a gel manicure at the salon, you can purchase a UV lamp and gel polish to do your own gel nails at home. This can save you a significant amount of money over time.

In conclusion, learning DIY hair and nail care can be a great way to save money on beauty salon expenses. While it may require some practice and investment in tools and products, the savings can add up quickly. With the right techniques and tools, you can keep your hair and nails looking great while still staying within your budget.

Number 97: Use a reusable nursing cover instead of disposables

Disposable nursing covers, also known as nursing pads or shields, are typically made of thin, absorbent materials that are designed to be thrown away after each use. While they may seem convenient, especially for moms on the go, their cost can add up quickly over time. Depending on the brand and quantity you purchase, disposable nursing covers can cost anywhere from a few cents to several dollars per unit. If you nurse your baby several times a day, every day, that cost can quickly become significant.

Reusable nursing covers, on the other hand, are made of durable, washable materials that can be used again and again. They often come in a variety of styles and designs, such as apron-style covers or infinity scarves, and can be found at a range of price points. While the upfront cost of a reusable nursing cover may be higher than a pack of disposable ones, it is a one-time investment that can save you money in the long run.

In addition to the cost savings, reusable nursing covers are also more environmentally friendly than their disposable counterparts. Because they can be washed and reused, they generate less waste and are a more sustainable option. Disposable nursing covers, on the other hand, can contribute to the growing problem of single-use plastic waste that is harming our planet.

Using a reusable nursing cover can also be more convenient and comfortable for nursing mothers. Many reusable covers are made of soft, breathable fabrics that can help regulate your body temperature and provide a more comfortable experience for both you and your baby. They also often have adjustable straps or ties that allow you to customize the fit and coverage to your liking.

Overall, choosing a reusable nursing cover instead of disposable ones can be a smart financial and environmental decision for new mothers. While the upfront cost may be higher, the long-term savings and benefits make it a worthwhile investment.

Number 98: Cut down appliance expenses

Energy-efficient products are designed to use less energy, which can translate into significant savings on your electricity bill. For instance, an energy-efficient refrigerator can save up to 40% on energy consumption compared to a traditional model. Similarly, an energy-efficient washing machine can save up to 50% on energy consumption. These savings can add up over time, and you can use the extra money to pay for other expenses or save for a rainy day.

When purchasing energy-efficient products, it is essential to look for the ENERGY STAR label. This label indicates that the product has met specific energy efficiency guidelines set by the US Environmental Protection Agency (EPA). ENERGY STAR products are designed to be more energy-efficient, which means that they use less energy to operate. This can translate into significant savings on your electricity bill over time.

Another way to cut down on home appliance expenses is to purchase appliances that are the right size for your needs. For example, if you live alone or with a partner, you don't need a massive refrigerator. Similarly, if you only do laundry once a week, you don't need a large washing machine. Purchasing appliances that are the right size for your needs can help you save on energy costs and reduce wasted space in your home.

Lastly, it is essential to maintain your appliances properly. Cleaning your refrigerator coils, for instance, can help it run more efficiently and save on energy costs. Similarly, cleaning your dryer's lint trap can help it run more efficiently and reduce the risk of a house fire. Proper maintenance of your appliances can help extend their lifespan, save you money on repairs, and reduce your energy costs.

In conclusion, cutting down on home appliance expenses can be achieved by purchasing energy-efficient products, buying appliances that are the right size for your needs, and maintaining your appliances properly. By implementing these practices, you can save money on your electricity bill, reduce your carbon footprint, and enjoy a more comfortable and sustainable lifestyle.

Number 99: Use a reusable make up brush instead of disposables

Makeup lovers know the struggle of constantly buying new makeup brushes. Not only can they be expensive, but they also contribute to environmental waste. That's why switching to reusable makeup brushes can be a great way to save money and help the planet at the same time.

Disposable makeup brushes are made to be tossed after a few uses. While they may seem convenient, they can add up in cost over time. A high-quality set of reusable makeup brushes may cost more upfront, but they can last for years with proper care. This means you won't have to constantly repurchase new brushes, saving you money in the long run.

Additionally, disposable makeup brushes contribute to environmental waste. Each year, millions of plastic makeup brushes end up in landfills, where they can take hundreds of years to decompose. By using reusable brushes, you can help reduce your carbon footprint and minimize your impact on the environment.

Reusable makeup brushes also offer a better application experience. Unlike disposable brushes, which are often made with low-quality bristles, reusable brushes can be made with high-quality materials that provide a smooth and flawless application. This means you'll get better results with each use, making your makeup look even more stunning.

When it comes to cleaning reusable brushes, it's important to take proper care of them to ensure they last as long as possible. Simply rinse them with warm water and a gentle soap, then let them air dry. By taking care of your brushes, you'll be able to use them for years to come, saving you even more money in the long run.

In conclusion, switching to reusable makeup brushes is a great way to save money and help the environment. By investing in a set of high-quality brushes and taking proper care of them, you'll be able to achieve a flawless application and reduce your impact on the planet. So next time you're in the market for new makeup brushes, consider making the switch to reusable ones.

Number 100: Cut down entertainment expenses by doing free stuff

Entertainment is an important part of life, but it can also be expensive. Many people struggle to keep up with the cost of entertainment, but there are ways to cut down on these expenses without sacrificing fun. One way to do this is by using free resources to save money.

There are many free resources available that can provide entertainment without breaking the bank. Here are some ways to cut down on entertainment expenses by using free resources:

1. Public libraries

Public libraries are a great resource for free entertainment. They offer books, magazines, music, movies, and more. You can borrow these items for a certain period of time without having to pay anything. This is a great way to save money on entertainment expenses.

2. Online resources

The internet is full of free resources that can provide entertainment. You can watch movies and TV shows on streaming sites like YouTube and Vimeo. You can also listen to music on streaming services like Spotify and Pandora. There are also many free online games that you can play, which can provide hours of entertainment.

3. Local events

Many cities and towns host free events throughout the year. These events can include concerts, festivals, and fairs. Check your local newspaper or online events calendar to see what events are happening in your area.

4. Hobbies

Hobbies can be a great source of entertainment without costing a lot of money. You can take up a new hobby like painting, knitting, or writing. These hobbies can provide hours of entertainment and can be done at home, which can save money on going out.

In conclusion, there are many free resources available that can provide entertainment without breaking the bank. Public libraries, online resources, local events, hobbies, and spending time with friends and family are all great ways to save money on entertainment expenses. By using these free resources, you can still have fun and enjoy life without worrying about the cost.

Number 101: Use a reusable eye mask instead of disposables

Disposable eye masks are a popular item in the market because of their convenience and affordability. However, the cost of using them can add up over time, not to mention the environmental impact they have. One solution to this problem is to switch to a reusable eye mask instead.

Reusable eye masks are made from materials that can be washed and used again and again, making them a more sustainable and cost-effective option in the long run. They come in a variety of materials, including cotton, silk, and polyester, and can be found in a range of designs and patterns.

One of the main benefits of using a reusable eye mask is that it can save you money in the long run. While a disposable eye mask may only cost a few dollars, using them regularly can quickly add up over time. In contrast, a reusable eye mask can be used multiple times without needing to be replaced, making it a more cost-effective option.

Another benefit of using a reusable eye mask is that it is better for the environment. Disposable eye masks are typically made from materials that are not biodegradable and can take hundreds of years to decompose. This means that they contribute to landfills and pollute the environment. Reusable eye masks, on the other hand, can be washed and reused, reducing the amount of waste produced.

Reusable eye masks are also more comfortable to wear than disposable ones. They are often made from soft materials that feel gentle on the skin, helping to improve sleep quality. Additionally, reusable eye masks can be adjusted to fit your head, ensuring that they stay in place throughout the night.

In conclusion, using a reusable eye mask instead of disposable ones is a smart choice for both your wallet and the environment. They are more cost-effective in the long run, better for the environment, and offer improved comfort.

Thank you!

Dear Reader,

Thank you so much for taking the time to read 101 Ways to Save Money. Saving money can be a daunting task, but with the right knowledge and tools, it can become an achievable goal.

I am glad that the book was able to provide you with some valuable insights and practical tips to help you achieve your financial goals.

Once again, thank you for your kind words and for choosing to read my book. I wish you all the best on your journey towards financial freedom.

Sincerely,

Aiden Green